Casenote Legal Briefs

Securities Regulation

Adaptable to courses utilizing Cox, Hillman, and Langevoort's casebook on Securities Regulation

NORMAN S. GOLDENBERG, SENIOR EDITOR
PETER TENEN, MANAGING EDITOR

STAFF WRITERS
LEE ACKERMAN
BILL CARERO
KENLYN KANOUSE
DAVID KNOBLOCK
DAVID KYLER
HOWARD MATHEWS
KEMP RICHARDSON
JAMES ROSENTHAL
CHRISTINE YOUKER

PUBLISHED BY CASENOTES PUBLISHING CO., INC. 1640 5th ST., SUITE 208 SANTA MONICA, CA 90401

Copyright © 1998 by Casenotes Publishing Co., Inc.
All rights reserved. No part of this book may be reproduced in any form or by any electronic or mechanical means including information storage and retrieval system without permission from the publisher.

ISBN 0-87457-206-1

FORMAT FOR THE CASENOTE LEGAL BRIEF

CASE CAPSULE: This boldface section (first three paragraphs) highlights the procedual nature of the case, a short summary of the facts, and the rule of law. This is an invaluable quick-review device designed to refresh the student's memory for classroom discussion and exam preparation.

NATURE OF CASE: This section identifies the form of action (e.g., breach of contract, negligence, battery), the type of proceeding (e.g., demurrer, appeal from trial court's jury instructions) and the relief sought (e.g., damages, injunction, criminal sanctions).

FACT SUMMARY: The fact summary is included to refresh the student's memory. It can be used as a quick reminder of the facts when the student is chosen by an instructor to brief a case.

CONCISE RULE OF LAW: This portion of the brief summarizes the general principle of law that the case illustrates. Like the fact summary, it is included to refresh the student's memory. It may be used for instant recall of the court's holding and for classroom discussion or home review.

FACTS: This section contains all relevant facts of the case, including the contentions of the parties and the lower court holdings. It is written in a logical order to give the student a clear understanding of the case. The plaintiff and defendant are identified by their proper names throughout and are always labeled with a (P) or (D).

ISSUE: The issue is a concise question that brings out the essence of the opinion as it relates to the section of the casebook in which the case appears. Both substantive and procedural issues are included if relevant to the decision.

HOLDING AND DECISION: This section offers a clear and in-depth discussion of the rule of the case and the court's rationale. It is written in easy-to-understand language. When relevant, it includes a thorough discussion of the exceptions listed by the court, the concurring and dissenting opinions, and the names of the judges.

CONCURRENCE / DISSENT: All concurrences and dissents are briefed whenever they are included by the casebook editor.

EDITOR'S ANALYSIS: This last paragraph gives the student a broad understanding of where the case "fits in" with other cases in the section of the book and with the entire course. It is a hornbook-style discussion indicating whether the case is a majority or minority opinion and comparing the principal case with other cases in the casebook. It may also provide analysis from restatements, uniform codes, and law review articles. The editor's analysis will prove to be invaluable to classroom discussion.

CROSS-REFERENCE TO OUTLINE: Wherever possible, following each case is a cross-reference linking the subject matter of the issue to the appropriate place in the *Casenote Law Outline*, which provides further information on the subject.

WINTER v. G.P. PUTNAM'S SONS
938 F.2d 1033 (1991).

NATURE OF CASE: Appeal from summary judgment in a products liability action.

FACT SUMMARY: Winter (P) relied on a book on mushrooms published by Putnam (D) and became critically ill after eating a poisonous mushroom.

CONCISE RULE OF LAW: Strict products liability is not applicable to the expressions contained within a book.

FACTS: Winter (P) purchased The Encyclopedia of Mushrooms, a book published by Putnam (D), to help in collecting and eating wild mushrooms. In 1988, Winter (P), relying on descriptions in the book, ate some wild mushrooms which turned out to be poisonous. Winter (P) became so ill he required a liver transplant. He brought a strict products liability action against Putnam (D), alleging that the book contained erroneous and misleading information that caused his injury. Putnam (D) responded that the information in the book was not a product for purposes of strict products liability, and the trial court granted its motion for summary judgment. The trial court also rejected Winter's (P) actions for negligence and misrepresentation. Winter (P) appealed.

ISSUE: Is strict products liability applicable to the expressions contained within a book?

HOLDING AND DECISION: (Sneed, J.) No. Strict products liability is not applicable to the expressions contained within a book. Products liability is geared toward tangible objects. The expression of ideas is governed by copyright, libel, and misrepresentation laws. The Restatement (Second) of Torts lists examples of the items that are covered by §402A strict liability. All are tangible items, such as tires or automobiles. There is no indication that the doctrine should be expanded beyond this area. Furthermore, there is a strong public interest in the unfettered exchange of ideas. The threat of liability without fault could seriously inhibit persons who wish to share thoughts and ideas with others. Although some courts have held that aeronautical charts are products for purposes of strict liability, these charts are highly technical tools which resemble compasses. The Encyclopedia of Mushrooms, published by Putnam (D), is a book of pure thought and expression and therefore does not constitute a product for purposes of strict liability. Additionally, publishers do not owe a duty to investigate the contents of books that they distribute. Therefore, a negligence action may not be maintained by Winter (P) against Putnam (D). Affirmed.

EDITOR'S ANALYSIS: This decision is in accord with the rulings in most jurisdictions. See Alm v. Nostrand Reinhold Co., Inc., 480 N.E. 2d 1263 (Ill. 1985). The court also stated that since the publisher is not a guarantor of the accuracy of an author's statements, an action for negligent misrepresentation could not be maintained. The elements of negligent misrepresentation are stated in § 311 of the Restatement (Second) of Torts.

[For more information on misrepresentation, see Casenote Law Outline on Torts, Chapter 12, § III, Negligent Misrepresentation.]

NOTE TO STUDENT

OUR GOAL. It is the goal of Casenotes Publishing Company, Inc. to create and distribute the finest, clearest and most accurate legal briefs available. To this end, we are constantly seeking new ideas, comments and constructive criticism. As a user of *Casenote Legal Briefs,* your suggestions will be highly valued. With all correspondence, please include your complete name, address, and telephone number, including area code and zip code.

THE TOTAL STUDY SYSTEM. Casenote Legal Briefs are just one part of the Casenotes TOTAL STUDY SYSTEM. Most briefs are (wherever possible) cross-referenced to the appropriate *Casenote Law Outline,* which will elaborate on the issue at hand. By purchasing a Law Outline together with your Legal Brief, you will have both parts of the Casenotes TOTAL STUDY SYSTEM. (See the advertising in the front of this book for a list of Law Outlines currently available.)

A NOTE ABOUT LANGUAGE. Please note that the language used in *Casenote Legal Briefs* in reference to minority groups and women reflects terminology used within the historical context of the time in which the respective courts wrote the opinions. We at Casenotes Publishing Co., Inc. are well aware of and very sensitive to the desires of all people to be treated with dignity and to be referred to as they prefer. Because such preferences change from time to time, and because the language of the courts reflects the time period in which opinions were written, our case briefs will not necessarily reflect contemporary references. We appreciate your understanding and invite your comments.

A NOTE REGARDING NEW EDITIONS. As of our press date, this Casenote Legal Brief is current and includes briefs of all cases in the current version of the casebook, divided into chapters that correspond to that edition of the casebook. However, occasionally a new edition of the casebook comes out in the interim, and sometimes the casebook author will make changes in the sequence of the cases in the chapters, add or delete cases, or change the chapter titles. Should you be using this Legal Brief in conjuction with a casebook that was issued later than this book, you can receive all of the newer cases, which are available free from us, by sending in the "Supplement Request Form" in this section of the book (please follow all instructions on that form). The Supplement(s) will contain all the missing cases, and will bring your Casenote Legal Brief up to date.

EDITOR'S NOTE. Casenote Legal Briefs are intended to supplement the student's casebook, not replace it. There is no substitute for the student's own mastery of this important learning and study technique. If used properly, *Casenote Legal Briefs* are an effective law study aid that will serve to reinforce the student's understanding of the cases.

REF# 1272-97-698

SUPPLEMENT REQUEST FORM

At the time this book was printed, a brief was included for every major case in the casebook and for every existing supplement to the casebook. However, if a new supplement to the casebook (or a new edition of the casebook) has been published since this publication was printed and if that casebook supplement (or new edition of the casebook) was available for sale at the time you purchased this Casenote Legal Briefs book, we will be pleased to provide you the new cases contained therein AT NO CHARGE when you send us a stamped, self-addressed envelope.

TO OBTAIN YOUR FREE SUPPLEMENT MATERIAL, **YOU MUST FOLLOW THE INSTRUCTIONS BELOW PRECISELY** OR YOUR REQUEST WILL NOT BE ACKNOWLEDGED!

1. Please check if there is in fact an existing supplement and, if so, that the cases are not already included in your Casenote Legal Briefs. Check the main table of cases as well as the supplement table of cases, if any.

2. **REMOVE THIS ENTIRE PAGE FROM THE BOOK.** You MUST send this ORIGINAL page to receive your supplement. This page acts as your proof of purchase and contains the reference number necessary to fill your supplement request properly. No photocopy of this page or written request will be honored or answered. Any request from which the reference number has been removed, altered or obliterated will not be honored.

3. Prepare a STAMPED self-addressed envelope for return mailing. Be sure to use a FULL SIZE (9 X 12) ENVELOPE (MANILA TYPE) so that the supplement will fit and AFFIX ENOUGH POSTAGE TO COVER 3 OZ. **ANY SUPPLEMENT REQUEST NOT ACCOMPANIED BY A STAMPED SELF-ADDRESSED ENVELOPE WILL ABSOLUTELY NOT BE FILLED OR ACKNOWLEDGED.**

4. MULTIPLE SUPPLEMENT REQUESTS: If you are ordering more than one supplement, we suggest that you enclose a stamped, self-addressed envelope for each supplement requested. If you enclose only one envelope for a multiple request, your order may not be filled immediately should any supplement which you requested still be in production. In other words, your order will be held by us until it can be filled completely.

5. Casenotes prints two kinds of supplements. A "New Edition" supplement is issued when a new edition of your casebook is published. A "New Edition" supplement gives you all major cases found in the new edition of the casebook which did not appear in the previous edition. A regular "supplement" is issued when a paperback supplement to your casebook is published. If the box at the lower right is stamped, then the "New Edition" supplement was provided to your bookstore and is *not* available from Casenotes; however, Casenotes will still send you any regular "supplements" which have been printed either before or after the new edition of your casebook appeared and which, according to the reference number at the top of this page, have not been included in this book. If the box is not stamped, Casenotes will send you any supplements, "New Edition" and/or regular, needed to completely update your Casenote Legal Briefs.

NOTE: REQUESTS FOR SUPPLEMENTS WILL NOT BE FILLED UNLESS THESE INSTRUCTIONS ARE COMPLIED WITH!

6. Fill in the following information:

Full title of CASEBOOK _____**SECURITIES REGULATION**_____

CASEBOOK author's name _____**Cox, Hillman, and Langevoort**_____

Copyright year of new edition or new paperback supplement __

Name and location of bookstore where this Casenote Legal Brief was purchased _____

Name and location of law school you attend _____

Any comments regarding Casenote Legal Briefs _____

NOTE: IF THIS BOX IS STAMPED, NO NEW EDITION SUPPLEMENT CAN BE OBTAINED BY MAIL.

PUBLISHED BY CASENOTES PUBLISHING CO., INC. 1640 5th ST, SUITE 208 SANTA MONICA, CA 90401

PLEASE PRINT
NAME _____ PHONE _____ DATE _____
ADDRESS/CITY/STATE/ZIP _____

Announcing the First *Totally Integrated* Law Study System

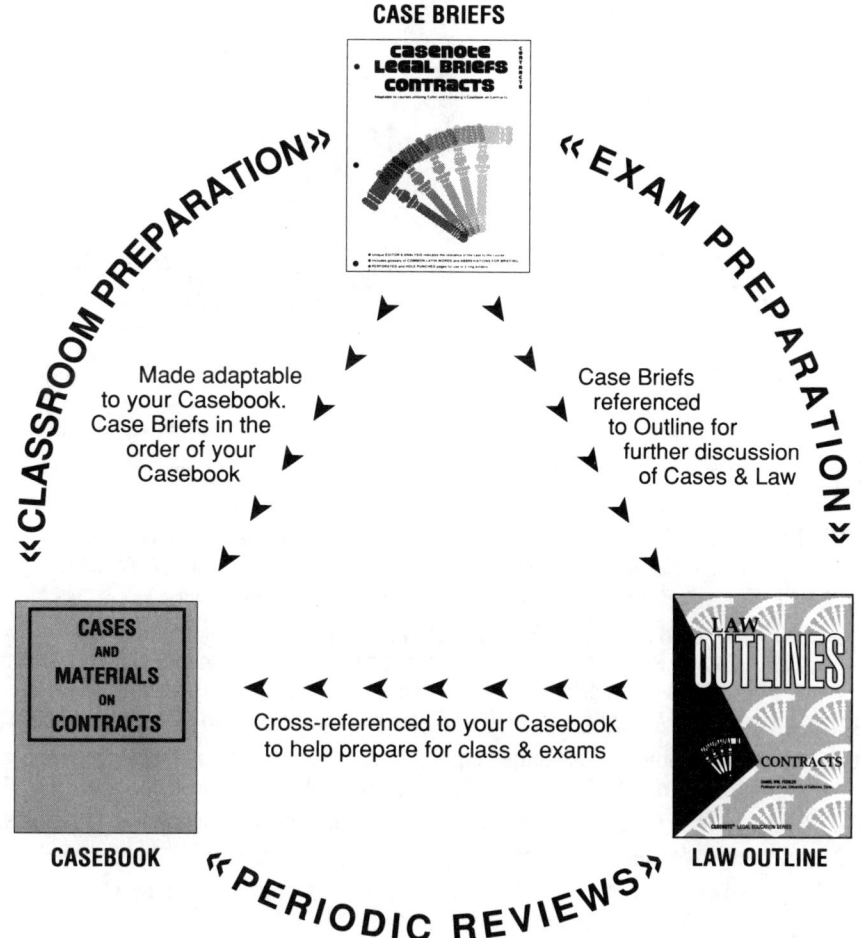

Casenotes Integrated Study System Makes Studying Easier and More Effective Than Ever!

Casenotes has just made studying easier and more effective than ever before, because we've done the work for you! Through our exclusive integrated study system, most briefs found in this volume of Casenote Legal Briefs are cross-referenced to the corresponding area of law in the Casenote Law Outline series. The cross-reference immediately follows the Editor's Analysis at the end of the brief, and it will direct you to the corresponding chapter and section number in the Casenote Law Outline for further information on the case or the area of law.

This cross-referencing feature will enable you to make the most effective use of your time. While each Casenote Law Outline focuses on a particular subject area of the law, each legal briefs volume is adapted to a specific casebook. Now, with cross-referencing of Casenote Legal Briefs to Casenote Law Outlines, you can have the best of both worlds – briefs for all major cases in your casebooks and easy-to-find, easy-to-read explanations of the law in our Law Outline series. Casenote Law Outlines are authored exclusively by law professors who are nationally recognized authorities in their field. So using Casenote Law Outlines is like studying with the top law professors.

Try Casenotes new totally integrated study system and see just how easy and effective studying can be.

Casenotes Integrated Study System Does The Work For You!

LAW OUTLINES from CASENOTE
the Ultimate Outline

- WRITTEN BY NATIONALLY RECOGNIZED AUTHORITIES IN THEIR FIELD.
- FEATURING A FLEXIBLE, SUBJECT-ORIENTED APPROACH.
- CONTAINS: TABLE OF CONTENTS; CAPSULE OUTLINE; FULL OUTLINE; EXAM PREPARATION; GLOSSARY; TABLE OF CASES; TABLE OF AUTHORITIES; CASEBOOK CROSS REFERENCE CHART; INDEX.
- THE TOTAL LAW SUMMARY UTILIZING THE MOST COMPREHENSIVE STUDY APPROACH IN THE MOST EFFECTIVE, EASY-TO-READ FORMAT.

REF #	SUBJECT / AUTHORS	RETAIL PRICE (effective 7/1/98)
#5260	ADMINISTRATIVE LAW by **Charles H. Koch, Jr.,** Dudley W. Woodbridge Professor of Law, College of William and Mary. **Sidney A. Shapiro,** John M. Rounds Professor of Law, University of Kansas. (1996 w/'98 supp.)	$20.95
#5040	CIVIL PROCEDURE by **John B. Oakley,** Professor of Law, University of California, Davis. **Rex R. Perschbacher,** Professor of Law & Associate Dean, Academic Affairs, University of California, Davis. (1996)	$21.95
	COMMERCIAL LAW (see 5700 SALES ● 5710 SECURED TRANS. ● 5720 NEG. INSTRUMENTS & PMT. SYST.)	
#5070	CONFLICT OF LAWS by **Luther L. McDougal, III,** W.R. Irby Professor of Law, Tulane University. **Robert L. Felix,** James P. Mozingo, III, Prof. of Law, Univ. of S. Carolina. (1996)	$20.95
#5080	CONSTITUTIONAL LAW by **Gary Goodpaster,** Prof. of Law, Univ. of California, Davis. (1997 w/'98 supp.)	$23.95
#5010	CONTRACTS by **Daniel Wm. Fessler,** Professor of Law, University of California, Davis. (1996)	$20.95
#5050	CORPORATIONS AND ALTERNATIVE BUSINESS VEHICLES by **Lewis D. Solomon,** Arthur Selwin Miller Research Prof. of Law, George Washington Univ. **Daniel Wm. Fessler,** Prof. of Law, University of California, Davis. **Arthur E. Wilmarth, Jr.,** Assoc. Prof. of Law, George Washington University. (1997)	$23.95
#5020	CRIMINAL LAW by **Joshua Dressler,** Professor of Law, McGeorge School of Law. (1996)	$20.95
#5200	CRIMINAL PROCEDURE by **Joshua Dressler,** Prof. of Law, McGeorge School of Law. (1997)	$19.95
#5800	ESTATE & GIFT TAX INCLUDING THE FEDERAL GENERATION-SKIPPING TAX by **Joseph M. Dodge,** W.H. Francis Prof. of Law, University of Texas at Austin (w/ supp. due Fall 1998)	$20.95
#5060	EVIDENCE by **Kenneth Graham, Jr.,** Professor of Law, University of California, Los Angeles. (1996)	$22.95
#5400	FEDERAL COURTS by **Howard P. Fink,** Isadore and Ida Topper Prof. of Law, Ohio State University. **Linda S. Mullenix,** Bernard J. Ward Centennial Prof. of Law, Univ. of Texas. (1997)	$21.95
#5210	FEDERAL INCOME TAXATION by **Joseph M. Dodge,** W.H. Francis Professor of Law, University of Texas at Austin (1998).	$21.95
#5300	LEGAL RESEARCH by **Nancy L. Schultz,** Associate Professor of Law, Chapman University. **Louis J. Sirico, Jr.,** Professor of Law, Villanova University. (1996)	$20.95
#5720	NEGOTIABLE INST. & PMT. SYST. by **Donald B. King,** Professor of Law, Saint Louis University. **Peter Winship,** James Cleo Thompson, Sr. Trustee Prof., SMU. (1995)	$21.95
#5030	PROPERTY by **Sheldon F. Kurtz,** Percy Bordwell Professor of Law, University of Iowa. **Patricia Cain,** Professor of Law, University of Iowa (1997)	$21.95
#5700	SALES by **Robert E. Scott,** Dean and Lewis F. Powell, Jr. Professor of Law, University of Virginia. **Donald B. King,** Professor of Law, Saint Louis University. (1992)	$20.95
#5710	SECURED TRANSACTIONS by **Donald B. King,** Professor of Law, Saint Louis University. (1995 w/'96 supp.)	$19.95
#5000	TORTS by **George C. Christie,** James B. Duke Professor of Law, Duke University. **Jerry J. Phillips,** W.P. Toms Professor of Law & Chair, Committee on Admissions, University of Tennessee. (1996 w/'98 supp.)	$21.95
#5220	WILLS, TRUSTS & ESTATES by **William M. McGovern,** Professor of Law, University of California, Los Angeles. (1996)	$21.95

rev. 6/1/98

CASENOTE LEGAL BRIEFS

PRICE LIST EFFECTIVE JULY 1, 1998 • PRICES SUBJECT TO CHANGE WITHOUT NOTICE

Ref. No.	Course	Adaptable to Courses Utilizing	Retail Price
1263	ADMINISTRATIVE LAW	BREYER, STEWART & SUNSTEIN	20.00
1266	ADMINISTRATIVE LAW	CASS, DIVER & BEERMAN	18.00
1260	ADMINISTRATIVE LAW	GELLHORN, B., S., R., S. & F.	18.00
1264	ADMINISTRATIVE LAW	MASHAW, MERRILL & SHANE	19.50
1267	ADMINISTRATIVE LAW	REESE	18.00
1262	ADMINISTRATIVE LAW	SCHWARTZ	19.00
1350	AGENCY & PARTNERSHIP (ENT.ORG)	CONARD, KNAUSS & SIEGEL	22.00
1351	AGENCY & PARTNERSHIP	HYNES	21.00
1690	AMERICAN INDIAN LAW	GETCHES, W. & W.	TBA
1281	ANTITRUST (TRADE REGULATION)	HANDLER, P., G. & W.	18.50
1280	ANTITRUST	AREEDA & KAPLOW	17.50
1283	ANTITRUST	SULLIVAN & HOVENKAMP	19.00
1611	BANKING LAW	MACEY & MILLER	18.00
1303	BANKRUPTCY (DEBTOR-CREDITOR)	EISENBERG	20.00
1305	BANKRUPTCY	JORDAN & WARREN	18.00
1058	BUSINESS ASSOCIATIONS (CORPORATIONS)	KLEIN & RAMSEYER	20.00
1040	CIVIL PROCEDURE	COUND, F., M. & S	21.00
1043	CIVIL PROCEDURE	FIELD, KAPLAN & CLERMONT	21.00
1049	CIVIL PROCEDURE	FREER & PERDUE	17.00
1041	CIVIL PROCEDURE	HAZARD, TAIT & FLETCHER	20.00
1047	CIVIL PROCEDURE	MARCUS, REDISH & SHERMAN	19.00
1044	CIVIL PROCEDURE	ROSENBERG, S. & D.	21.00
1046	CIVIL PROCEDURE	YEAZELL	18.00
1311	COMM'L LAW	FARNSWORTH, H., R., H. & M.	20.00
1312	COMM'L LAW	JORDAN & WARREN	20.00
1310	COMM'L LAW (SALES/SEC.TR./PAY.LAW [Sys.])	SPEIDEL, SUMMERS & WHITE	23.00
1313	COMM'L LAW (SALES/SEC.TR./PAY.LAW)	WHALEY	21.00
1320	COMMUNITY PROPERTY	BIRD	18.50
1630	COMPARATIVE LAW	SCHLESINGER, B., D., H & W.	17.00
1048	COMPLEX LITIGATION	MARCUS & SHERMAN	18.00
1072	CONFLICTS	BRILMAYER	18.00
1071	CONFLICTS	CRAMTON, C. K., & K.	18.00
1070	CONFLICTS	ROSENBERG, HAY & W.	21.00
1086	CONSTITUTIONAL LAW	BREST & LEVINSON	19.00
1082	CONSTITUTIONAL LAW	COHEN & VARAT	22.00
1088	CONSTITUTIONAL LAW	FARBER, ESKRIDGE & FRICKEY	19.00
1080	CONSTITUTIONAL LAW	GUNTHER & SULLIVAN	21.00
1081	CONSTITUTIONAL LAW	LOCKHART, K., C., S. & F.	19.00
1085	CONSTITUTIONAL LAW	ROTUNDA	19.00
1089	CONSTITUTIONAL LAW (FIRST AMENDMENT)	SHIFFRIN & CHOPER	16.00
1087	CONSTITUTIONAL LAW	STONE, S., S. & T.	20.00
1103	CONTRACTS	BARNETT	22.00
1102	CONTRACTS	BURTON	21.00
1017	CONTRACTS	CALAMARI, PERILLO & BENDER	24.00
1101	CONTRACTS	CRANDALL & WHALEY	21.00
1014	CONTRACTS	DAWSON, HARVEY & H.	20.00
1010	CONTRACTS	FARNSWORTH & YOUNG	19.00
1011	CONTRACTS	FULLER & EISENBERG	22.00
1100	CONTRACTS	HAMILTON, RAU & WEINTRAUB	20.00
1013	CONTRACTS	KESSLER, GILMORE & KRONMAN	24.00
1016	CONTRACTS	KNAPP & CRYSTAL	21.50
1012	CONTRACTS	MURPHY & SPEIDEL	23.00
1018	CONTRACTS	MURRAY	23.00
1015	CONTRACTS	ROSETT	22.00
1019	CONTRACTS	VERNON	21.00
1502	COPYRIGHT	GOLDSTEIN	19.00
1501	COPYRIGHT	NIMMER, M. M. & N.	20.50
1218	CORPORATE TAXATION	LIND, S. L. & R	15.00
1050	CORPORATIONS	CARY & EISENBERG	20.00
1054	CORPORATIONS	CHOPER, COFFEE, & GILSON	22.50
1350	CORPORATIONS (ENTERPRISE ORG.)	CONARD, KNAUSS & SIEGEL	22.00
1053	CORPORATIONS	HAMILTON	20.00
1058	CORPORATIONS (BUSINESS ASSOCIATIONS)	KLEIN & RAMSEYER	20.00
1057	CORPORATIONS	O'KELLEY & THOMPSON	19.00
1056	CORPORATIONS	SOLOMON, S., B. & W.	20.00
1052	CORPORATIONS	VAGTS	19.00
1300	CREDITOR'S RIGHTS (DEBTOR-CREDITOR)	RIESENFELD	22.00
1550	CRIMINAL JUSTICE	WEINREB	19.00
1029	CRIMINAL LAW	BONNIE, C., J. & L.	18.00
1020	CRIMINAL LAW	BOYCE & PERKINS	23.00
1028	CRIMINAL LAW	DRESSLER	22.00
1027	CRIMINAL LAW	JOHNSON	21.00
1021	CRIMINAL LAW	KADISH & SCHULHOFER	20.00
1026	CRIMINAL LAW	KAPLAN, WEISBERG & BINDER	19.00
1205	CRIMINAL PROCEDURE	ALLEN, KUHNS & STUNTZ	18.00
1202	CRIMINAL PROCEDURE	HADDAD, Z., S. & B.	21.00
1200	CRIMINAL PROCEDURE	KAMISAR, LAFAVE & ISRAEL	20.00
1204	CRIMINAL PROCEDURE	SALTZBURG & CAPRA	18.00
1203	CRIMINAL PROCEDURE (PROCESS)	WEINREB	19.50
1303	DEBTOR-CREDITOR	EISENBERG	20.00
1300	DEBTOR-CREDITOR (CRED. RTS.)	RIESENFELD	22.00
1304	DEBTOR-CREDITOR	WARREN & WESTBROOK	20.00
1224	DECEDENTS ESTATES (TRUSTS)	RITCHIE, A. & E.(DOBRIS & STERK)	22.00
1222	DECEDENTS ESTATES	SCOLES & HALBACH	22.50
1231	DECEDENTS ESTATES (TRUSTS)	WAGGONER, A. & F.	21.00
	DOMESTIC RELATIONS (see FAMILY LAW)		
3000	EDUCATION LAW (COURSE OUTLINE)	AQUILA & PETZKE	26.50
1670	EMPLOYMENT DISCRIMINATION	FRIEDMAN & STRICKLER	18.00
1671	EMPLOYMENT DISCRIMINATION	ZIMMER, SULLIVAN, R. & C.	19.00
1660	EMPLOYMENT LAW	ROTHSTEIN, KNAPP & LIEBMAN	20.50
1350	ENTERPRISE ORGANIZATION	CONARD, KNAUSS & SIEGEL	22.00
1342	ENVIRONMENTAL LAW	ANDERSON, MANDELKER & T.	17.00
1341	ENVIRONMENTAL LAW	FINDLEY & FARBER	19.00
1345	ENVIRONMENTAL LAW	MENELL & STEWART	18.00
1344	ENVIRONMENTAL LAW	PERCIVAL, MILLER, S. & L.	19.00
1343	ENVIRONMENTAL LAW	PLATER, A., G. & G.	18.00
	EQUITY (see REMEDIES)		

Ref. No.	Course	Adaptable to Courses Utilizing	Retail Price
1217	ESTATE & GIFT TAXATION	BITTKER, CLARK & McCOUCH	16.00
	ETHICS (see PROFESSIONAL RESPONSIBILITY)		
1065	EVIDENCE	GREEN & NESSON	21.00
1066	EVIDENCE	MUELLER & KIRKPATRICK	18.00
1064	EVIDENCE	STRONG, BROUN & M.	23.50
1062	EVIDENCE	SUTTON & WELLBORN	23.00
1061	EVIDENCE	WALTZ & PARK	21.00
1060	EVIDENCE	WEINSTEIN, M., A. & B.	23.50
1244	FAMILY LAW (DOMESTIC RELATIONS)	AREEN	23.00
1242	FAMILY LAW (DOMESTIC RELATIONS)	CLARK & GLOWINSKY	20.00
1245	FAMILY LAW (DOMESTIC RELATIONS)	ELLMAN, KURTZ & BARTLETT	21.00
1246	FAMILY LAW (DOMESTIC RELATIONS)	HARRIS, T. & W.	20.00
1243	FAMILY LAW (DOMESTIC RELATIONS)	KRAUSE, O., E. & G.	25.00
1240	FAMILY LAW (DOMESTIC RELATIONS)	WADLINGTON	21.00
1231	FAMILY PROPERTY LAW (WILLS/TRUSTS)	WAGGONER, A. & F.	21.00
1360	FEDERAL COURTS	FALLON, M. & S. (HART & W.)	20.00
1360	FEDERAL COURTS	HART & WECHSLER (FALLON)	20.00
1363	FEDERAL COURTS	LOW & JEFFRIES	17.00
1361	FEDERAL COURTS	McCORMICK, C. W.	21.00
1364	FEDERAL COURTS	REDISH & SHERRY	18.00
1089	FIRST AMENDMENT (CONSTITUTIONAL LAW)	SHIFFRIN & CHOPER	16.00
1510	GRATUITOUS TRANSFERS	CLARK, LUSKY & MURPHY	19.00
1650	HEALTH LAW	FURROW, J., J. & S.	18.50
1640	IMMIGRATION LAW	ALEINIKOFF, MARTIN & M.	17.00
1641	IMMIGRATION LAW	LEGOMSKY	20.00
1690	INDIAN LAW (AMERICAN)	GETCHES, W. & W.	TBA
1371	INSURANCE LAW	KEETON	22.00
1372	INSURANCE LAW	YORK, WHELAN & MARTINEZ	20.00
1370	INSURANCE LAW	YOUNG & HOLMES	18.00
1394	INTERNATIONAL BUSINESS TRANSACTIONS	FOLSOM, GORDON & SPANOGLE	16.00
1393	INTERNATIONAL LAW	CARTER & TRIMBLE	17.00
1392	INTERNATIONAL LAW	HENKIN, P., S. & S.	18.00
1390	INTERNATIONAL LAW	OLIVER, F., B. S. & W.	23.00
1331	LABOR LAW	COX, BOK, GORMAN & FINKIN	20.00
1332	LABOR LAW	HARPER & ESTREICHER	21.00
1333	LABOR LAW	LESLIE	19.50
1330	LABOR LAW	MERRIFIELD, S. & C.	20.00
1471	LAND FINANCE (REAL ESTATE TRANS)	BERGER & JOHNSTONE	19.00
1620	LAND FINANCE (REAL ESTATE TRANS)	NELSON & WHITMAN	20.00
1452	LAND USE	CALLIES, FREILICH & ROBERTS	18.00
1421	LEGISLATION	ESKRIDGE & FRICKEY	16.00
1480	MASS MEDIA	FRANKLIN & ANDERSON	16.00
1312	NEGOTIABLE INSTRUMENTS (COMM. LAW)	JORDAN & WARREN	20.00
1541	OIL & GAS	KUNTZ, L, A. & S.	19.00
1540	OIL & GAS	MAXWELL, WILLIAMS, M. & K.	19.00
1560	PATENT LAW	FRANCIS & COLLINS	24.00
1310	PAYMENT LAW [SYST.][COMM. LAW]	SPEIDEL, SUMMERS & WHITE	23.00
1313	PAYMENT LAW (COMM.LAW / NEG. INST.)	WHALEY	23.00
1431	PRODUCTS LIABILITY	OWEN, MONTGOMERY & K.	23.00
1091	PROF. RESPONSIBILITY (ETHICS)	GILLERS	14.00
1093	PROF. RESPONSIBILITY (ETHICS)	HAZARD, KONIAK, & CRAMTON	19.00
1092	PROF. RESPONSIBILITY (ETHICS)	MORGAN & ROTUNDA	14.00
1030	PROPERTY	CASNER & LEACH	22.00
1031	PROPERTY	CRIBBET, J., F. & S.	22.50
1037	PROPERTY	DONAHUE, KAUPER & MARTIN	19.00
1035	PROPERTY	DUKEMINIER & KRIER	19.00
1034	PROPERTY	HAAR & LIEBMAN	21.50
1036	PROPERTY	KURTZ & HOVENKAMP	20.00
1033	PROPERTY	NELSON, STOEBUCK, & W.	21.50
1032	PROPERTY	RABIN & KWALL	21.00
1038	PROPERTY	SINGER	19.50
1621	REAL ESTATE TRANSACTIONS	GOLDSTEIN & KORNGOLD	19.00
1471	REAL ESTATE TRANS. & FIN. (LAND FINANCE)	BERGER & JOHNSTONE	19.00
1620	REAL ESTATE TRANSFER & FINANCE	NELSON & WHITMAN	19.00
1254	REMEDIES (EQUITY)	LAYCOCK	21.00
1253	REMEDIES (EQUITY)	LEAVELL, L., N. & K/F	22.00
1252	REMEDIES (EQUITY)	RE & RE	24.00
1255	REMEDIES (EQUITY)	SHOBEN & TABB	23.50
1250	REMEDIES (EQUITY)	YORK, BAUMAN & RENDLEMAN	26.00
1310	SALES (COMM. LAW)	SPEIDEL, SUMMERS & WHITE	23.00
1313	SALES (COMM. LAW)	WHALEY	21.00
1312	SECURED TRANS. (COMM. LAW)	JORDAN & WARREN	20.00
1310	SECURED TRANS.	SPEIDEL, SUMMERS & WHITE	23.00
1313	SECURED TRANS. (COMM. LAW)	WHALEY	21.00
1272	SECURITIES REGULATION	COX, HILLMAN, LANGEVOORT	19.00
1270	SECURITIES REGULATION	JENNINGS, M., C. & S.	19.00
1680	SPORTS LAW	WEILER & ROBERTS	18.50
1217	TAXATION (ESTATE & GIFT)	BITTKER, CLARK & McCOUCH	16.00
1219	TAXATION (INDIV. INC.)	BURKE & FRIEL	20.00
1212	TAXATION (FED. INC.)	FREELAND, LIND & STEPHENS	19.00
1211	TAXATION (FED. INC.)	GRAETZ & SCHENK	18.00
1210	TAXATION (FED. INC.)	KLEIN & BANKMAN	19.00
1218	TAXATION (CORPORATE)	LIND, S., L. & R.	15.00
1006	TORTS	DOBBS	20.00
1003	TORTS	EPSTEIN	21.50
1004	TORTS	FRANKLIN & RABIN	18.50
1001	TORTS	HENDERSON, P. & S.	21.50
1000	TORTS	PROSSER, W., S., K. & P.	25.00
1005	TORTS	SHULMAN, JAMES & GRAY	23.00
1281	TRADE REGULATION (ANTITRUST)	HANDLER, P., G. & W.	18.50
1230	TRUSTS	BOGERT, O., H. & H.	21.50
1231	TRUSTS/WILLS (FAMILY PROPERTY LAW)	WAGGONER, A. & F.	21.00
1410	U.C.C.	EPSTEIN, MARTIN, H. & N.	16.00
1223	WILLS, TRUSTS & ESTATES	DUKEMINIER & JOHANSON	20.00
1220	WILLS	MECHEM & ATKINSON	21.00
1231	WILLS/TRUSTS (FAMILY PROPERTY LAW)	WAGGONER, A. & F.	21.00

(SERIES XLI)

CASENOTES PUBLISHING CO. INC. ● 1640 FIFTH STREET, SUITE 208 ● SANTA MONICA, CA 90401 ● (310) 395-6500

E-Mail Address- casenote@westworld.com
Website-http://www.casenotes.com

PLEASE PURCHASE FROM YOUR LOCAL BOOKSTORE. IF UNAVAILABLE, YOU MAY ORDER DIRECT.*
4TH CLASS POSTAGE (ALLOW TWO WEEKS) $1.00 PER ORDER; 1ST CLASS POSTAGE $3.00 (ONE BOOK), $2.00 EACH (TWO OR MORE BOOKS)
*CALIF. RESIDENTS PLEASE ADD 8¼% SALES TAX

Notes

GLOSSARY
COMMON LATIN WORDS AND PHRASES ENCOUNTERED IN LAW

A FORTIORI: Because one fact exists or has been proven, therefore a second fact that is related to the first fact must also exist.

A PRIORI: From the cause to the effect. A term of logic used to denote that when one generally accepted truth is shown to be a cause, another particular effect must necessarily follow.

AB INITIO: From the beginning; a condition which has existed throughout, as in a marriage which was void ab initio.

ACTUS REUS: The wrongful act; in criminal law, such action sufficient to trigger criminal liability.

AD VALOREM: According to value; an ad valorem tax is imposed upon an item located within the taxing jurisdiction calculated by the value of such item.

AMICUS CURIAE: Friend of the court. Its most common usage takes the form of an amicus curiae brief, filed by a person who is not a party to an action but is nonetheless allowed to offer an argument supporting his legal interests.

ARGUENDO: In arguing. A statement, possibly hypothetical, made for the purpose of argument, is one made arguendo.

BILL QUIA TIMET: A bill to quiet title (establish ownership) to real property.

BONA FIDE: True, honest, or genuine. May refer to a person's legal position based on good faith or lacking notice of fraud (such as a bona fide purchaser for value) or to the authenticity of a particular document (such as a bona fide last will and testament).

CAUSA MORTIS: With approaching death in mind. A gift causa mortis is a gift given by a party who feels certain that death is imminent.

CAVEAT EMPTOR: Let the buyer beware. This maxim is reflected in the rule of law that a buyer purchases at his own risk because it is his responsibility to examine, judge, test, and otherwise inspect what he is buying.

CERTIORARI: A writ of review. Petitions for review of a case by the United States Supreme Court are most often done by means of a writ of certiorari.

CONTRA: On the other hand. Opposite. Contrary to.

CORAM NOBIS: Before us; writs of error directed to the court that originally rendered the judgment.

CORAM VOBIS: Before you; writs of error directed by an appellate court to a lower court to correct a factual error.

CORPUS DELICTI: The body of the crime; the requisite elements of a crime amounting to objective proof that a crime has been committed.

CUM TESTAMENTO ANNEXO, ADMINISTRATOR (ADMINISTRATOR C.T.A.): With will annexed; an administrator c.t.a. settles an estate pursuant to a will in which he is not appointed.

DE BONIS NON, ADMINISTRATOR (ADMINISTRATOR D.B.N.): Of goods not administered; an administrator d.b.n. settles a partially settled estate.

DE FACTO: In fact; in reality; actually. Existing in fact but not officially approved or engendered.

DE JURE: By right; lawful. Describes a condition that is legitimate "as a matter of law," in contrast to the term "de facto," which connotes something existing in fact but not legally sanctioned or authorized. For example, de facto segregation refers to segregation brought about by housing patterns, etc., whereas de jure segregation refers to segregation created by law.

DE MINIMUS: Of minimal importance; insignificant; a trifle; not worth bothering about.

DE NOVO: Anew; a second time; afresh. A trial de novo is a new trial held at the appellate level as if the case originated there and the trial at a lower level had not taken place.

DICTA: Generally used as an abbreviated form of obiter dicta, a term describing those portions of a judicial opinion incidental or not necessary to resolution of the specific question before the court. Such nonessential statements and remarks are not considered to be binding precedent.

DUCES TECUM: Refers to a particular type of writ or subpoena requesting a party or organization to produce certain documents in their possession.

EN BANC: Full bench. Where a court sits with all justices present rather than the usual quorum.

EX PARTE: For one side or one party only. An ex parte proceeding is one undertaken for the benefit of only one party, without notice to, or an appearance by, an adverse party.

EX POST FACTO: After the fact. An ex post facto law is a law that retroactively changes the consequences of a prior act.

EX REL.: Abbreviated form of the term ex relatione, meaning, upon relation or information. When the state brings an action in which it has no interest against an individual at the instigation of one who has a private interest in the matter.

FORUM NON CONVENIENS: Inconvenient forum. Although a court may have jurisdiction over the case, the action should be tried in a more conveniently located court, one to which parties and witnesses may more easily travel, for example.

GUARDIAN AD LITEM: A guardian of an infant as to litigation, appointed to represent the infant and pursue his/her rights.

HABEAS CORPUS: You have the body. The modern writ of habeas corpus is a writ directing that a person (body) being detained (such as a prisoner) be brought before the court so that the legality of his detention can be judicially ascertained.

IN CAMERA: In private, in chambers. When a hearing is held before a judge in his chambers or when all spectators are excluded from the courtroom.

IN FORMA PAUPERIS: In the manner of a pauper. A party who proceeds in forma pauperis because of his poverty is one who is allowed to bring suit without liability for costs.

INFRA: Below, under. A word referring the reader to a later part of a book. (The opposite of supra.)

IN LOCO PARENTIS: In the place of a parent.

IN PARI DELICTO: Equally wrong; a court of equity will not grant requested relief to an applicant who is in pari delicto, or as much at fault in the transactions giving rise to the controversy as is the opponent of the applicant.

IN PARI MATERIA: On like subject matter or upon the same matter. Statutes relating to the same person or things are said to be in pari materia. It is a general rule of statutory construction that such statutes should be construed together, i.e., looked at as if they together constituted one law.

IN PERSONAM: Against the person. Jurisdiction over the person of an individual.

IN RE: In the matter of. Used to designate a proceeding involving an estate or other property.

IN REM: A term that signifies an action against the res, or thing. An action in rem is basically one that is taken directly against property, as distinguished from an action in personam, i.e., against the person.

INTER ALIA: Among other things. Used to show that the whole of a statement, pleading, list, statute, etc., has not been set forth in its entirety.

INTER PARTES: Between the parties. May refer to contracts, conveyances or other transactions having legal significance.

INTER VIVOS: Between the living. An inter vivos gift is a gift made by a living grantor, as distinguished from bequests contained in a will, which pass upon the death of the testator.

IPSO FACTO: By the mere fact itself.

JUS: Law or the entire body of law.

LEX LOCI: The law of the place; the notion that the rights of parties to a legal proceeding are governed by the law of the place where those rights arose.
MALUM IN SE: Evil or wrong in and of itself; inherently wrong. This term describes an act that is wrong by its very nature, as opposed to one which would not be wrong but for the fact that there is a specific legal prohibition against it (malum prohibitum).
MALUM PROHIBITUM: Wrong because prohibited, but not inherently evil. Used to describe something that is wrong because it is expressly forbidden by law but that is not in and of itself evil, e.g., speeding.
MANDAMUS: We command. A writ directing an official to take a certain action.
MENS REA: A guilty mind; a criminal intent. A term used to signify the mental state that accompanies a crime or other prohibited act. Some crimes require only a general mens rea (general intent to do the prohibited act), but others, like assault with intent to murder, require the existence of a specific mens rea.
MODUS OPERANDI: Method of operating; generally refers to the manner or style of a criminal in committing crimes, admissible in appropriate cases as evidence of the identity of a defendant.
NEXUS: A connection to.
NISI PRIUS: A court of first impression. A nisi prius court is one where issues of fact are tried before a judge or jury.
N.O.V. (NON OBSTANTE VEREDICTO): Notwithstanding the verdict. A judgment n.o.v. is a judgment given in favor of one party despite the fact that a verdict was returned in favor of the other party, the justification being that the verdict either had no reasonable support in fact or was contrary to law.
NUNC PRO TUNC: Now for then. This phrase refers to actions that may be taken and will then have full retroactive effect.
PENDENTE LITE: Pending the suit; pending litigation underway.
PER CAPITA: By head; beneficiaries of an estate, if they take in equal shares, take per capita.
PER CURIAM: By the court; signifies an opinion ostensibly written "by the whole court" and with no identified author.
PER SE: By itself, in itself; inherently.
PER STIRPES: By representation. Used primarily in the law of wills to describe the method of distribution where a person, generally because of death, is unable to take that which is left to him by the will of another, and therefore his heirs divide such property between them rather than take under the will individually.
PRIMA FACIE: On its face, at first sight. A prima facie case is one that is sufficient on its face, meaning that the evidence supporting it is adequate to establish the case until contradicted or overcome by other evidence.
PRO TANTO: For so much; as far as it goes. Often used in eminent domain cases when a property owner receives partial payment for his land without prejudice to his right to bring suit for the full amount he claims his land to be worth.
QUANTUM MERUIT: As much as he deserves. Refers to recovery based on the doctrine of unjust enrichment in those cases in which a party has rendered valuable services or furnished materials that were accepted and enjoyed by another under circumstances that would reasonably notify the recipient that the rendering party expected to be paid. In essence, the law implies a contract to pay the reasonable value of the services or materials furnished.
QUASI: Almost like; as if; nearly. This term is essentially used to signify that one subject or thing is almost analogous to another but that material differences between them do exist. For example, a quasi-criminal proceeding is one that is not strictly criminal but shares enough of the same characteristics to require some of the same safeguards (e.g., procedural due process must be followed in a parol hearing).
QUID PRO QUO: Something for something. In contract law, the consideration, something of value, passed between the parties to render the contract binding.
RES GESTAE: Things done; in evidence law, this principle justifies the admission of a statement that would otherwise be hearsay when it is made so closely to the event in question as to be said to be a part of it, or with such spontaneity as not to have the possibility of falsehood.
RES IPSA LOQUITUR: The thing speaks for itself. This doctrine gives rise to a rebuttable presumption of negligence when the instrumentality causing the injury was within the exclusive control of the defendant, and the injury was one that does not normally occur unless a person has been negligent.
RES JUDICATA: A matter adjudged. Doctrine which provides that once a court of competent jurisdiction has rendered a final judgment or decree on the merits, that judgment or decree is conclusive upon the parties to the case and prevents them from engaging in any other litigation on the points and issues determined therein.
RESPONDEAT SUPERIOR: Let the master reply. This doctrine holds the master liable for the wrongful acts of his servant (or the principal for his agent) in those cases in which the servant (or agent) was acting within the scope of his authority at the time of the injury.
STARE DECISIS: To stand by or adhere to that which has been decided. The common law doctrine of stare decisis attempts to give security and certainty to the law by following the policy that once a principle of law as applicable to a certain set of facts has been set forth in a decision, it forms a precedent which will subsequently be followed, even though a different decision might be made were it the first time the question had arisen. Of course, stare decisis is not an inviolable principle and is departed from in instances where there is good cause (e.g., considerations of public policy led the Supreme Court to disregard prior decisions sanctioning segregation).
SUPRA: Above. A word referring a reader to an earlier part of a book.
ULTRA VIRES: Beyond the power. This phrase is most commonly used to refer to actions taken by a corporation that are beyond the power or legal authority of the corporation.

ADDENDUM OF FRENCH DERIVATIVES

IN PAIS: Not pursuant to legal proceedings.
CHATTEL: Tangible personal property.
CY PRES: Doctrine permitting courts to apply trust funds to purposes not expressed in the trust but necessary to carry out the settlor's intent.
PER AUTRE VIE: For another's life; in property law, an estate may be granted that will terminate upon the death of someone other than the grantee.
PROFIT A PRENDRE: A license to remove minerals or other produce from land.
VOIR DIRE: Process of questioning jurors as to their predispositions about the case or parties to a proceeding in order to identify those jurors displaying bias or prejudice.

HOW TO BRIEF A CASE

A. DECIDE ON A FORMAT AND STICK TO IT

Structure is essential to a good brief. It enables you to arrange systematically the related parts that are scattered throughout most cases, thus making manageable and understandable what might otherwise seem to be an endless and unfathomable sea of information. There are, of course, an unlimited number of formats that can be utilized. However, it is best to find one that suits your needs and stick to it. Consistency breeds both efficiency and the security that when called upon you will know where to look in your brief for the information you are asked to give.

Any format, as long as it presents the essential elements of a case in an organized fashion, can be used. Experience, however, has led *Casenotes* to develop and utilize the following format because of its logical flow and universal applicability.

NATURE OF CASE: This is a brief statement of the legal character and procedural status of the case (e.g., "Appeal of a burglary conviction").

There are many different alternatives open to a litigant dissatisfied with a court ruling. The key to determining which one has been used is to discover *who is asking this court for what.*

This first entry in the brief should be kept as *short as possible.* The student should use the court's terminology if the student understands it. But since jurisdictions vary as to the titles of pleadings, the best entry is the one that apprises the student of who wants what in this proceeding, not the one that sounds most like the court's language.

CONCISE RULE OF LAW: A statement of the general principle of law that the case illustrates (e.g., "An acceptance that varies any term of the offer is considered a rejection and counteroffer").

Determining the rule of law of a case is a procedure similar to determining the issue of the case. Avoid being fooled by red herrings; there may be a few rules of law mentioned in the case excerpt, but usually only one is *the* rule with which the casebook editor is concerned. The techniques used to locate the issue, described below, may also be utilized to find the rule of law. Generally, your best guide is simply the chapter heading. It is a clue to the point the casebook editor seeks to make and should be kept in mind when reading every case in the respective section.

FACTS: A synopsis of only the essential facts of the case, i.e., those bearing upon or leading up to the issue.

The facts entry should be a short statement of the events and transactions that led one party to initiate legal proceedings against another in the first place. While some cases conveniently state the salient facts at the beginning of the decision, in other instances they will have to be culled from hiding places throughout the text, even from concurring and dissenting opinions. Some of the "facts" will often be in dispute and should be so noted. Conflicting evidence may be briefly pointed up. "Hard" facts must be included. Both must be *relevant* in order to be listed in the facts entry. It is impossible to tell what is relevant until the entire case is read, as the ultimate determination of the rights and liabilities of the parties may turn on something buried deep in the opinion.

The facts entry should never be longer than one to three *short* sentences.

It is often helpful to identify the role played by a party in a given context. For example, in a construction contract case the identification of a party as the "contractor" or "builder" alleviates the need to tell that that party was the one who was supposed to have built the house.

It is always helpful, and a good general practice, to identify the "plaintiff" and the "defendant." This may seem elementary and uncomplicated, but, especially in view of the creative editing practiced by some casebook editors, it is sometimes a difficult or even impossible task. Bear in mind that the *party presently* seeking something from this court may not be the plaintiff, and that sometimes only the cross-claim of a defendant is treated in the excerpt. Confusing or misaligning the parties can ruin your analysis and understanding of the case.

ISSUE: A statement of the general legal question answered by or illustrated in the case. For clarity, the issue is best put in the form of a question capable of a "yes" or "no" answer. In reality, the issue is simply the Concise Rule of Law put in the form of a question (e.g., "May an offer be accepted by performance?").

The major problem presented in discerning what is *the* issue in the case is that an opinion usually purports to raise and answer several questions. However, except for rare cases, only one such question is really the issue in the case. Collateral issues not necessary to the resolution of the matter in controversy are handled by the court by language known as *"obiter dictum"* or merely *"dictum."* While dicta may be included later in the brief, it has no place under the issue heading.

To find the issue, the student again asks *who wants what* and then goes on to ask *why did that party succeed or fail in getting it.* Once this is determined, the "why" should be turned into a question.

The complexity of the issues in the cases will vary, but in all cases a single-sentence question should sum up the issue. *In a few cases,* there will be two, or even more rarely, three issues of equal importance to the resolution of the case. Each should be expressed in a single-sentence question.

Since many issues are resolved by a court in coming to a final disposition of a case, the casebook editor will reproduce the portion of the opinion containing the issue or issues most relevant to the area of law under scrutiny. A noted law professor gave this advice: "Close the book; look at the title on the cover." Chances are, if it is Property, the student need not concern himself with whether, for example, the federal government's treatment of the plaintiff's land really raises a federal question sufficient to support jurisdiction on this ground in federal court.

The same rule applies to chapter headings designating sub-areas within the subjects. They tip the student off as to what the text is designed to teach. The cases are arranged in a casebook to show a progression or development of the law, so that the preceding cases may also help.

It is also most important to remember to *read the notes and questions* at the end of a case to determine what the editors wanted the student to have gleaned from it.

HOLDING AND DECISION: This section should succinctly explain the rationale of the court in arriving at its decision. In capsulizing the "reasoning" of the court, it should always include an application of the general rule or rules of law to the specific facts of the case. Hidden justifications come to light in this entry; the reasons for the state of the law, the public policies, the biases and prejudices, those considerations that influence the justices' thinking and, ultimately, the outcome of the case. At the end, there should be a short indication of the disposition or procedural resolution of the case (e.g., "Decision of the trial court for Mr. Smith (P) reversed").

The foregoing format is designed to help you "digest" the reams of case material with which you will be faced in your law school career. Once mastered by practice, it will place at your fingertips the information the authors of your casebooks have sought to impart to you in case-by-case illustration and analysis.

B. BE AS ECONOMICAL AS POSSIBLE IN BRIEFING CASES

Once armed with a format that encourages succinctness, it is as important to be economical with regard to the time spent on the actual reading of the case as it is to be economical in the writing of the brief itself. This does not mean "skimming" a case. Rather, it means reading the case with an "eye" trained to recognize into which "section" of your brief a particular passage or line fits and having a system for quickly and precisely marking the case so that the passages fitting any one particular part of the brief can be easily identified and brought together in a concise and accurate manner when the brief is actually written.

It is of no use to simply repeat everything in the opinion of the court; the student should only record enough information to trigger his or her recollection of what the court said. Nevertheless, an accurate statement of the "law of the case," i.e., the legal principle applied to the facts, is absolutely essential to class preparation and to learning the law under the case method.

To that end, it is important to develop a "shorthand" that you can use to make margin notations. These notations will tell you at a glance in which section of the brief you will be placing that particular passage or portion of the opinion.

Some students prefer to underline all the salient portions of the opinion (with a pencil or colored underliner marker), making marginal notations as they go along. Others prefer the color-coded method of underlining, utilizing different colors of markers to underline the salient portions of the case, each separate color being used to represent a different section of the brief. For example, blue underlining could be used for passages relating to the concise rule of law, yellow for those relating to the issue, and green for those relating to the holding and decision, etc. While it has its advocates, the color-coded method can be confusing and time-consuming (all that time spent on changing colored markers). Furthermore, it can interfere with the continuity and concentration many students deem essential to the reading of a case for maximum comprehension. In the end, however, it is a matter of personal preference and style. Just remember, whatever method you use, underlining must be used sparingly or its value is lost.

For those who take the marginal notation route, an efficient and easy method is to go along underlining the key portions of the case and placing in the margin alongside them the following "markers" to indicate where a particular passage or line "belongs" in the brief you will write:

N	(NATURE OF CASE)
CR	(CONCISE RULE OF LAW)
I	(ISSUE)
HC	(HOLDING AND DECISION, relates to the CONCISE RULE OF LAW behind the decision)
HR	(HOLDING AND DECISION, gives the RATIONALE or reasoning behind the decision)
HA	(HOLDING AND DECISION, APPLIES the general principle(s) of law to the facts of the case to arrive at the decision)

Remember that a particular passage may well contain information necessary to more than one part of your brief, in which case you simply note that in the margin. If you are using the color-coded underlining method instead of margin notation, simply make asterisks or checks in the margin next to the passage in question in the colors that indicate the additional sections of the brief where it might be utilized.

The economy of utilizing "shorthand" in marking cases for briefing can be maintained in the actual brief writing process itself by utilizing "law student shorthand" within the brief. There are many commonly used words and phrases for which abbreviations can be substituted in your briefs (and in your class notes also). You can develop abbreviations that are personal to you and which will save you a lot of time. A reference list of briefing abbreviations will be found elsewhere in this book.

C. USE BOTH THE BRIEFING PROCESS AND THE BRIEF AS A LEARNING TOOL

Now that you have a format and the tools for briefing cases efficiently, the most important thing is to make the time spent in briefing profitable to you and to make the most advantageous use of the briefs you create. Of course, the briefs are invaluable for classroom reference when you are called upon to explain or analyze a particular case. However, they are also useful in reviewing for exams. A quick glance at the fact summary should bring the case to mind, and a rereading of the concise rule of law should enable you to go over the underlying legal concept in your mind, how it was applied in that particular case, and how it might apply in other factual settings.

As to the value to be derived from engaging in the briefing process itself, there is an immediate benefit that arises from being forced to sift through the essential facts and reasoning from the court's opinion and to succinctly express them in your own words in your brief. The process ensures that you understand the case and the point that it illustrates, and that means you will be ready to absorb further analysis and information brought forth in class. It also ensures you will have something to say when called upon in class. The briefing process helps develop a mental agility for getting to the *gist* of a case and for identifying, expounding on, and applying the legal concepts and issues found there. Of most immediate concern, that is the mental process on which you must rely in taking law school examinations. Of more lasting concern, it is also the mental process upon which a lawyer relies in serving his clients and in making his living.

CASENOTE LEGAL BRIEFS — SECURITIES REGULATION

TABLE OF CASES

A
Aaron v. SEC 45
Ackerberg v. Johnson 32
Akerman v. Oryx Communications Inc. 41

B
Backman v. Polaroid Corp. 53
Banco Espanol De Credito v. Security Pacific
  Nat'l Bank 18
Basic, Inc. v. Levinson 3
Basic, Inc. v. Levinson 58
Bateman Eichler, Hill Richards, Inc. v. Berner 87
Bateman Eichler, Hill Richards, Inc. v. Berner ... 100
Bersch v. Drexel Firestone, Inc. 111
Bonny v. The Society of Lloyd's 114
Brown v. E.F. Hutton Group Inc. 97
Busch v. Carpenter 24

C
Carpenter v. United States 84
Carter and Johnson, In re 91
CBI Industries v. Horton 66
Central Bank of Denver, N.A. v. First Interstate
  Bank of Denver, N.A. 88
Chiarella v. United States 62
Cowin v. Bresler 56
CTS Corp. v. Dynamics Corp. of America 79

D
Dirks v. SEC 63
Donohoe v. Consolidated Operating
  & Production Corp. 89
Doran v. Petroleum Management Corp. 26

E
Epstein v. MCA Corp. 76
Escott v. Barchris Construction Co. 40

F
Feit v. Leasco Data Processing Equipment Corp. 21
Franchard Corporation, In the Matter of 5

G
Gartenberg v. Merrill Lynch Asset Management Inc. 105
Gould v. American-Hawaiian Steamship Co. 70
Gustafson v. Alloyd Co. 43

H
Hanly v. SEC 96
Hocking v. Dubois 11
Huddleston v. Herman & MacLean 57

I
International Brotherhood of Teamsters, Chauffeurs, Warehousemen & Helpers of America v. Daniel 13

J
John Gutfreund et al., In the Matter of 95
Jordan v. Duff & Phelps, Inc. 55

K
Kaufman v. Trump's Castle Funding 4
Keating, Muething & Klekamp, In re 92
Kenman Corp., In the Matter of 28
Koch v. Hankins 16

L
Landreth Timber Co. v. Landreth 15
Lowe v. SEC 103

M
Mai Basic Four Inc. v. Prime Computer Inc. ... 75
Marine Bank v. Weaver 14
Mark v. FSC Securities Corp. 27
Mashburn v. National Healthcare, Inc. 85
Merrill Lynch, Pierce, Fenner
  & Smith v. Arceneaux 98
Meyers Parking System, Inc., In re 72

N
National Association of Securities
  Dealers, Inc., In re 20

O
Otto v. Variable Annuity Life Insurance Co. ... 38

P
Pinter v. Dahl 42

R
R. William Bradford, In the Matter of 82
R.M. Perez & Associates, Inc. v. Welch 99
Regional Properties, Inc. v. Financial & Real Estate
  Consulting Co. 86
Reves v. Ernst & Young 17
Robert Jautz, In re 94
Roberts v. Peat, Marwick, Mitchell & Co. 87
Rowe v. Maremont Corp. 59

S
Sanders v. John Nuveen & Co. 44
Schoenbaum v. Firstbrook 110

Continued on next page

Notes

TABLE OF CASES (Continued)

Schreiber v. Burlington Northern, Inc. 78
SEC v. Capital Gains Research Bureau, Inc. 102
SEC v. Carter Hawley Hale Stores, Inc. 77
SEC v. Children's Hospital 36
SEC v. Chinese Consolidated Benevolent
    Association, Inc. 30
SEC v. Datronics Engineers, Inc. 34
SEC v. Fifth Avenue Coach Lines, Inc. 107
SEC v. Kasser 112
SEC v. Koscot Interplanetary, Inc. 9
SEC v. Jos. Schlitz Brewing Co. 6
SEC v. Manor Nursing Centers, Inc. 22
SEC v. Midwest Technical Development Corp. 106
SEC v. National Student Marketing Corp. 90
SEC v. Ralston Purina Co. 25
SEC v. Texas Gulf Sulphur Co. 52
SEC v. Variable Annuity Life Insurance Co.
    Of America 37
SEC v. W.J. Howey Co. 8
SEC v. Wall Street Publishing Institute 104
SEC v. World-wide Coin Investments LTD. 49

T
Texas International Airlines v. National Airlines Inc. 67
Time Warner, Inc. Securities Litigation, In re 54

U
United Housing Foundation, Inc. v. Forman 12
United States v. Bryan 65
United States v. Carpenter 64
United States v. Dixon 83
United States v. Mulheren 48
United States v. Wolfson 31

V
Virginia Bankshares, Inc. v. Sandberg 71

W
Wals v. Fox Hills Development Corporation 10
Washington Public Power Supply System
    Securities Litigation, In re 46
Wellman v. Dickinson 74
Wielgos v. Commonwealth Edison Co. 2

Z
Zoelsch v. Arthur Andersen & Co. 113

CHAPTER 2*
INQUIRIES INTO THE MATERIALITY OF INFORMATION

QUICK REFERENCE RULES OF LAW

1. **The "Total Mix" of Information and Market Efficiency.** Cost projections in SEC filings are forward-looking statements that may not form the basis for a fraud claim unless they are made without a reasonable basis. (Wielgos v. Commonwealth Edison Co.)

2. **Speculative Information and Materiality.** The materiality of preliminary merger discussions for purposes of Rule 10b-5 violations depends on the anticipated magnitude of the merger and its probability. (Basic, Inc. v. Levinson)

3. **"Bespeaks Caution" and the Safe Harbor for Forward-Looking Statements.** Cautionary language in a prospectus, if sufficient, renders alleged omissions or misrepresentations immaterial as a matter of law. (Kaufman v. Trump's Castle Funding)

4. **Disclosure Beyond the Bottom Line: Management Integrity.** An issuer must disclose all information that reveals the quality of management since that factor is an essential ingredient in an informed investment decision and hence, a material fact. (In the Matter of Franchard Corp.)

5. **The Materiality of Violations of State or Federal Law.** The failure to disclose illegal activities is material for purposes of Rule 10b-5. (SEC v. Jos. Schlitz Brewing Co.)

*There are no cases in Chapter 1.

WIELGOS v. COMMONWEALTH EDISON CO.
892 F.2d 509 (7th Cir. 1989).

NATURE OF CASE: Appeal from the dismissal of a class action for violations of federal securities laws.

FACT SUMMARY: Wielgos (P) filed a class action on behalf of investors who bought Edison (D) shares in a shelf offering because Edison (D) had underestimated the costs of completing a nuclear reactor.

CONCISE RULE OF LAW: Cost projections in SEC filings are forward-looking statements that may not form the basis for a fraud claim unless they are made without a reasonable basis.

FACTS: In September 1983, Commonwealth Edison (D) put three million shares of common stock "on the shelf" according to Rule 415 in order to hold the stock for deferred sale. Edison's (D) registration statement incorporated many other SEC filings and a prospectus including cost projections for the nuclear reactors Edison (D) had under construction. In December 1983, Wielgos (P) bought 500 shares of Edison at market price. In January 1983, the Atomic Safety and Licensing Board (ASLB) rejected Edison's (D) request for a license for the Byron I reactor. Edison's (D) stock prices dropped dramatically, and Wielgos (P) filed a class-action suit for the amount that the equity securities declined in price after purchase. Wielgos (P) asserted that Edison (D) had misrepresented the cost of completing the Byron I reactor and had omitted the fact that the ASLB was in the process of considering the application at the time of the shelf offering. The trial court ruled that Edison's (D) cost projections could not be the basis of a fraud claim and that the omission of the license application status was not material. Wielgos (P) appealed.

ISSUE: May cost projections in SEC filings form the basis for a fraud claim?

HOLDING AND DECISION: (Easterbrook, J.) No. Cost projections in SEC filings are forward-looking statements that may not form the basis for a fraud claim unless they are made without a reasonable basis. Material errors in a prospectus that is filed with the SEC are generally sufficient to prove liability. However, SEC Rule 175 provides that forward-looking statements containing projections of revenues or costs made by the issuers of securities may not be deemed fraudulent. This rule provides a safe harbor for incorrect statements unless they are made without a reasonable basis or are disclosed without good faith. Rule 175 assumes that investors are sophisticated and can understand the limits of predictions. The rule does not require the issuer to reveal the assumptions that are the basis of the projections. Although Edison's (D) statements regarding the costs of Byron I were inaccurate, they had a reasonable basis because they were estimated according to an assumption that everything would proceed without complications. Item 103 of Regulation S-K requires issuers to disclose pending legal proceedings except for ordinary routine litigation incidental to business. Edison (D) disclosed that the Byron I reactor was not licensed. Edison (D) was not required to print statements as to the pending ASLB application because information already in the public domain advised investors that costs would rise if a license was denied. Therefore, Edison's (D) omission of the ASLB pending application was not material. Affirmed.

EDITOR'S ANALYSIS: Other courts have agreed that information already in the public domain can override omissions in SEC filings. In Seaboard World Airlines v. Tiger Intl., Inc., 600 F.2d 355 (2nd Cir. 1979), the court held that Tiger's statements regarding the liquidation value of Seaboard could not be materially misleading because prior SEC filings had revealed a dispute between the companies regarding the liquidation value. Note also that the fact that a forecast, in hindsight, turns out to be untrue does not necessarily make it untrue, or fraudulent, when made.

NOTES:

BASIC, INC. v. LEVINSON
485 U.S. 224 (1988).

NATURE OF CASE: Appeal from reversal of summary judgment in a class action for violation of Rule 10b-5.

FACT SUMMARY: Basic (D) made misleading statements about merger negotiations which former shareholders (P) contended violated Rule 10b-5.

CONCISE RULE OF LAW: The materiality of preliminary merger discussions for purposes of Rule 10b-5 violations depends on the anticipated magnitude of the merger and its probability.

FACTS: In 1976, Combustion Engineering began to take steps to acquire Basic (D), a company that manufactured chemical refractories. Combustion officers met with Basic (D) officers and directors concerning the possibility of a merger. However, Basic (D) proceeded to make three public statements, including a reply to an inquiry by the New York Stock Exchange, denying that it was involved in merger negotiations. On December 18, 1978, Basic (D) finally released a statement that it had been "approached" about a merger. The next day, the Basic (D) board endorsed Combustion's offer of $46 per share. Former shareholders (P) of Basic (D) who had sold their stock after Basic's (D) first statement denying merger negotiations filed a class action for violations of § 10(b) of the 1934 Securities Exchange Act and Rule 10b-5. Rule 10b-5 bars false or misleading material statements in regard to securities trading. Basic (D) responded that the statements were not material because it was possible that the merger would not take place. The trial court granted summary judgment to Basic (D), but the court of appeals reversed. Basic (D) appealed.

ISSUE: May statements regarding preliminary merger discussions be material for purposes of Rule 10b-5?

HOLDING AND DECISION: (Blackmun, J.) Yes. The materiality of preliminary merger discussions for purposes of Rule 10b-5 violations depends on the anticipated magnitude of the merger and its probability. In order to prevail on a Rule 10b-5 claim, a plaintiff must show that the statements were misleading as to a "material" fact. A fact is material under Rule 10b-5 if there is a substantial likelihood that a reasonable shareholder would consider the disclosure or omission of the fact to have significantly altered the total mix of information available. Since preliminary merger negotiations often fail, it is difficult to determine whether a reasonable investor would consider the information significant at the time. Therefore, the determination must be made in light of the particular facts of each case. The size of the corporations involved and the potential premiums over market value are proper considerations in deciding whether the magnitude of a merger is significant. This fact-specific inquiry is adopted over a bright-line rule where merger discussions do not become material until an agreement-in-principle is reached. Such a rule does not reflect the purpose of federal securities laws, i.e., to encourage disclosure of relevant information. The case is remanded to determine the anticipated magnitude of the merger and the probability of its occurrence at the time of Basic's (D) misleading statements.

EDITOR'S ANALYSIS: On remand, the court of appeals determined that summary judgment for Basic (D) was not appropriate given the test set by this decision. The Court's magnitude/probability test makes it very difficult for a defendant to win a summary judgment motion on materiality in Rule 10b-5 cases. There will not often be statements which a court can declare immaterial as a matter of law, given the use of such a fact-specific inquiry to determine the significance of information to a reasonable investor.

NOTES:

KAUFMAN v. TRUMP'S CASTLE FUNDING
7 F.3d 357 (3d Cir. 1993).

NATURE OF CASE: Appeal from dismissal of a complaint in an action related to the issuance of mortgage investment bonds.

FACT SUMMARY: Kaufman (P) and others who had invested in a public bond offering issued in conjunction with the purchase of a partially completed casino/hotel filed suit, alleging that the prospectus issued with the bond offering contained material misrepresentations and omissions.

CONCISE RULE OF LAW: Cautionary language in a prospectus, if sufficient, renders alleged omissions or misrepresentations immaterial as a matter of law.

FACTS: Trump's Castle Funding (D) made a public offering of first mortgage investment bonds in order to raise capital to purchase the Taj Mahal, a partially-completed casino/hotel. The prospectus accompanying the bonds contained general and specific warnings about the risks inherent in the project but also stated that the Partnership (D) believed that funds generated from the operation of the Taj Mahal would cover all of its debt service, both interest and principal. After learning that Trump's Castle (D) planned to file a Chapter 11 bankruptcy, Kaufman (P) and other bond investors filed separate complaints, alleging that the above statement was materially misleading because the partrnership (D) did not truthfully believe that it would be able to repay the bondholders. Therefore, the prospectus contained material misrepresentations and omissions in violation of the 1933 and 1934 Securities Acts. The district court dismissed the complaint for failure to state a claim. Kaufman (P) appealed.

ISSUE: Does cautionary language in a prospectus, if sufficient, render alleged omissions or misrepresentations immaterial as a matter of law?

HOLDING AND DECISION: (Becker, J.) Yes. Cautionary language in a prospectus, if sufficient, renders alleged omissions or misrepresentations immaterial as a matter of law. Because of the abundant and meaningful cautionary language contained in the prospectus, Kaufman (P) and the other investors have failed to state an actionable claim regarding the statement that the Partnership believed it could repay the bonds. The cautionary statements were tailored precisely to address the uncertainty concerning the Partnership's (D) prospective ability to repay the bondholders. A reasonable investor, having read these cautionary explanations, would understand that the Taj Mahal carried substantial risks. Given this context, no reasonable jury could conclude that the projection materially influenced a reasonable investor. Dismissal affirmed.

EDITOR'S ANALYSIS: The Third Circuit Court in the above case applied what has come to be known as the "bespeaks caution" doctrine. In doing so, it followed a number of appellate courts of appeals that have dismissed securities fraud claims under Rule 12(b)(6) because cautionary language in the offering document negated the materiality of an alleged misrepresentation or omission. However, a vague or blanket (boilerplate) disclaimer merely warning the reader that the investment has risks will ordinarily be inadequate to prevent misinformation.

NOTES:

IN THE MATTER OF FRANCHARD CORPORATION
42 SEC 163 (1964).

NATURE OF CASE: Hearing on a stop order motion.

FACT SUMMARY: Glickman transferred money from Franchard Corp. to one wholly owned corp. and pledged his controlling stock without informing the directors or disclosing the information in the registration statements.

CONCISE RULE OF LAW: An issuer must disclose all information that reveals the quality of management since that factor is an essential ingredient in an informed investment decision and hence, a material fact.

FACTS: Louis J. Glickman, a real estate developer and the impetus in the formation of many wholly owned corporations, caused the formation of Franchard Corp. (D) and controlled it by acquiring a majority of its authorized "B" shares. He exercised a dominant role in the management of its affairs. Three registration statements were filed becoming effective on October 12, 1960, October 2, 1961, and December 1, 1961 respectively. The 1960 prospectus stated that Glickman advanced substantial sums to other businesses that were to become subsidiaries of the registrant and that he had given money to the registrant. All sums were to be repaid without interest. After the effective date, Glickman transferred funds from the registrant to one of his wholly owned corporations. By the effective date of the second registration, the aggregate amount withdrawn from Franchard (D) was $2,372,511. Neither the 1961 prospectuses nor any of the amendments to the 1960 filing referred to these withdrawals. All prospectuses stated that Glickman owned most of Franchard's B shares as well as a large block of A. As of the effective date of the 1960 filing, these shares were unencumbered; however, shortly thereafter Glickman began to pledge those shares to finance his personal real estate ventures. By August 1961 all of the B stock and most of the A was securing loans up to $4 million with interest rates as high as 24%. The two 1961 filings made no mention of these loans. In May 1962, Franchard's board discovered the transfers. Glickman assured the board the transfers would stop and agreed to repay the money with 6% interest. However, Glickman made other withdrawals, and the directors retained a U.S. district court judge to determine Glickman's liability. The judge found that, although Glickman repaid the money at 6% interest, such interest was inadequate and that Glickman owed more money. This sum was never paid. The board learned that Glickman continued to withdraw funds from Franchard (D), that all of his and his wife's Franchard stock was pledged, and that Glickman and the wholly owned corporation to whom he had given the funds were in financial trouble. Glickman resigned and sold all of his B stock and some of his class A stock. Franchard (D) contended that disclosure of Glickman's transfers and pledges would be an unwarranted revelation of personal affairs and that the withdrawals were not material since they never exceeded 1.5% of the gross book value of Franchard assets.

ISSUE: Is the quality of management a material fact that must be disclosed in the registration statements filed by an issuer?

HOLDING AND DECISION: (Cary, J.) Yes. The quality of management is a material fact that must be disclosed in the registration statement to comply with the securities acts. This essential ingredient of informed investment decision is aided by the requirement that the issuer disclose management's past business experiences, the company's past financial status, any conflict of interest on the part of insiders that may conflict with their duty of loyalty to the corporation, the renumeration paid or proposed to be paid to management, and material transactions between the corporation, its officers, directors and holders of more than 10% stock and their associates. Glickman's transactions were material not only because of the substantial sums involved but also because they displayed Glickman's managerial ability and personal integrity. Since the offering was based on Glickman's reputation, information on his activities is material for many reasons: (1) it would reveal his strained financial position, (2) it is germane to an evaluation of his integrity, which is always material but even more so in view of Glickman's dominance and the relationship to his wholly owned corporation, (3) because Franchard (D) was operated on a cash flow basis and because of Glickman's need for cash, he had a powerful motive to maintain high distribution rates and high prices for the A shares; (4) the possible loss of control due to the pledges holds material significance since it was Glickman's reputation and control of Franchard (D) which induced investment. Disclosure remains a requirement even though the directors do not know of the transgressions. Congressional determination was that an issuer should not pass the loss to investors regardless of the diligence used to prepare a statement. Ordinarily a stop order would issue in such a case, but distributing copies of this opinion to past and present stockholders will be enough since Glickman has departed, transferring his controlling B shares to management, and registrants disclosures prior to these proceedings and the filing of amendments to the 1960 statements were a bona fide attempt to comply, and the publication containing the true facts was sent to Franchard stockholders.

EDITOR'S ANALYSIS: Additional situations which must be set forth in a registration statement are: (1) restrictions on disposition of earned surplus, (2) general risks inherent in the business (3) recent drop in business volume, (4) recent government regulations possibly affecting the business, (5) pending or threatened litigation including securities litigation, (6) conflict over patents, (7) proposed new business, (8) competitive conditions in the industry, and (9) operating plans for one year for companies without earnings history. The SEC now requires that the preliminary prospectus include: (1) estimated offering price and the factors used to arrive at the price, (2) the number of shares offered, and (3) the underwriting commission.

SEC v. JOS. SCHLITZ BREWING CO.
452 F. Supp. 824 (E.D. Wis. 1978).

NATURE OF CASE: Motion to dismiss an action against practices violating federal securities laws.

FACT SUMMARY: The SEC (P) contended that Schlitz (D) was required to disclose a nationwide illegal scheme to induce retailers to purchase Schlitz (D) products.

CONCISE RULE OF LAW: The failure to disclose illegal activities is material for purposes of Rule 10b-5.

FACTS: Schlitz (D) participated in an illegal scheme to induce retailers to purchase Schlitz (D) products by making payment to them in violation of the Federal Alcohol Administration Act (FAAA). Schlitz (D) also falsified its books with regard to the payments made within the scheme. Furthermore, the financial statements, periodic reports, and proxy solicitation material filed with the SEC (P) were incorrect due to the scheme. The SEC (P) filed suit contending that these false statements violated § 10(b) of the Securities Exchange Act of 1934 and Rule 10b-5. Schlitz (D) responded that the SEC (P) did not have jurisdiction because a grand jury had indicted Schlitz (D) regarding the violation of the FAAA. Schlitz (D) also argued that the information about its potentially illegal activities was not material.

ISSUE: Is the failure to disclose illegal activities material for purposes of Rule 10b-5?

HOLDING AND DECISION: (Gordon, J.) Yes. The failure to disclose illegal activities is material for purposes of Rule 10b-5. On the jurisdiction issue, more than one governmental agency may investigate the same conduct in order to bring simultaneous civil and criminal actions, as long as the respective remedies are not mutually exclusive. Therefore, the SEC (P) is not precluded from pursuing federal securities violations against Schlitz (D) even though a criminal action is also being pursued. Thus, the SEC (P) does have jurisdiction. In regard to Schlitz's (D) second line of defense, information must be disclosed when it is "material." Information is "material" if there is a substantial likelihood that a reasonable investor would attach importance to the matter in making investment decisions. For example, information that has a direct bearing on the integrity of management would be important to a reasonable investor. Also, although the dollar amount of illegal payments may be relatively small, such payments can be material if a larger amount of business is dependent or affected by them. The illegal activities of Schlitz (D) have a bearing on the integrity of the directors of the company. Furthermore, although the payments were relatively small in comparison to total revenues, the payments could affect valuable licenses to sell liquor that would in turn have great economic importance to Schlitz (D). Therefore, the information would certainly be important to reasonable investors and is, therefore, material. Schlitz' (D) motion to dismiss is denied.

EDITOR'S ANALYSIS: The SEC (P) has discovered that questionable payment practices or bribery nearly always results in falsified corporate books and records. Cash is usually accumulated in a manner that bypasses any accounting system. Thus, the SEC (P) maintains that bribery in any amount is an important factor in determining materiality because the practice casts doubt on the integrity of a company's records.

NOTES:

CHAPTER 3
THE DEFINITION OF A SECURITY

QUICK REFERENCE RULES OF LAW

1. **The Development of a Framework for Defining an Investment Contract.** An investment contract within the meaning of § 2(a) is a contract, transaction or scheme whereby money is invested in a common enterprise with profits derived solely from the efforts of others. (SEC v. W.J. Howey Co.)

2. **Howey Applied.** An investment contract will be found where the efforts of those other than the investor are the essential and significant managerial efforts, which affect the failure or success of the enterprise as a whole. (SEC v. Koscot Interplanetary, Inc.)

3. **Howey Applied.** A pooling of interests between the developer and each individual investor and also among the investors themselves is required to convert a sale of real estate to a sale of an investment contract. (Wals v. Fox Hills Development Corp.)

4. **Real Estate as Securities.** A real estate purchase constitutes purchase of a security for purposes of antifraud provisions where the investor has no power of control over the management of a common enterprise. (Hocking v. Dubois)

5. **Nonprofit Housing Cooperatives.** Commercial transactions in stock do not constitute securities under the Securities Acts where the purpose of the transaction is not to invest for profit. (United Housing Foundation v. Forman)

6. **Pension Plans.** Noncontributory, compulsory pension plans are not "securities" and therefore are not subject to the various requirements of the Securities Acts. (International Brotherhood of Teamsters, Chauffeurs, Warehousemen & Helpers of America v. Daniel)

7. **Context Considerations: Bank Certificates of Deposit and Privately Negotiated Investments.** A unique certificate of deposit issued by a federally regulated bank does not constitute a security under the antifraud provisions of the federal securities laws. (Marine Bank v. Weaver)

8. **Stock as a Security.** A sale of shares of stock will be covered by the securities laws, irrespective of the nature of the stockholder's role in managing the corporation. (Landreth Timber Co. v. Landreth)

9. **Partnership Interests as Securities.** Interests in general partnerships may be classified as securities when investors are prevented from exercising meaningful control over their investment. (Koch v. Hankins)

10. **Notes as Securities.** Promissory notes with immediate maturity qualify as securities when they are offered and sold to members of the public who seek to invest for profit. (Reves v. Ernst & Young)

11. **Beyond Reves: Loan Participations as Securities.** Loan participations, i.e., the practice of selling loans to other institutions, are not "securities." (Banco Espanol de Credito v. Security Pacific National Bank)

SEC v. W.J. HOWEY CO.
328 U.S. 293 (1946).

NATURE OF CASE: Action for injunction for violation of § 5(a) of the 1933 Act.

FACT SUMMARY: Company sold acreage to various investors together with a servicing contract for upkeep to be performed by one of its affiliate companies.

CONCISE RULE OF LAW: An investment contract within the meaning of § 2(a) is a contract, transaction or scheme whereby money is invested in a common enterprise with profits derived solely from the efforts of others.

FACTS: W.J. Howey (D) and Howey-in-the-Hills Service, Inc. (D) were Florida corporations under common control. Howey Co. owned large citrus acreage in Florida and annually offered one-half of 500 planted acres to the public. Each prospective purchaser was offered a land sales contract and a service contract whereby Howey Service was given a ten-year service contract, without option of cancellation, and whereby they were given a leasehold interest in the acreage with full and complete possession. They alone had authority to cultivate and harvest the groves. Although each prospective purchaser was free to hire his own service company, the sale literature stressed Howey Service and 85% of the acreage sold was covered by service contracts with Howey Service. A purchaser could not enter the property to market the crop, nor could they specify the fruit to be marketed. The company alone was accountable only for an allocation of net profits. Both lower courts determined that the contracts and deeds were separate transactions entailing only a sale of real estate; the circuit court ruled that there is no investment where the enterprise is not speculative or promotional in character and the tangible interest has intrinsic value independent from the success of the enterprise as a whole.

ISSUE: Is an investment contract whereby the prospective purchaser invests money in a common scheme to derive profits solely from the actions of others within the meaning of § 2(a)?

HOLDING AND DECISION: Yes. Although the term "investment contract" is not defined by the Act, many states used it in "Blue Sky" laws existing prior to adoption of the act. State courts have interpreted it to mean a scheme or device for payment of money intended to secure income or profit from its use. When the term "investment contract" was included in Section 2(a), Congress did so against this prior interpretation, and such a meaning is both reasonable and consistent with the statutory aims. Thus, "investment contract" means a contract, transaction, or scheme whereby a person invests money in a common enterprise to achieve profits solely from the efforts of others. Thus, it is immaterial whether the interests in the enterprise are evidenced by certificates or by interests in the physical assets used in the enterprise. The transactions here are clearly within the term in that what was offered was not a fee simple interest in land with a management service but rather an opportunity to persons unequipped to develop the land to share in profits derived by the efforts of a company whose equipment and personnel make it the essential ingredient in the investment. Here, the land sales contract and deeds only show each owner's interest in the profits and the transfer of land is incidental. The test enunciated by the court of appeals is unrealistic in that if the test be met it is immaterial whether the enterprise is speculative or whether the sale of property is or is not of intrinsic value.

DISSENT: (Frankfurter, J.) The issue critical here is whether contracts for land and contracts for management of land were separate agreements or one transaction, and this is a question of fact, which was found not to be. Under the federal two-court rule, this case should not come within the statute.

EDITOR'S ANALYSIS: The test formulated in Howey has been the one most consistently applied by all federal courts, with the greatest amount of attention being directed to defining what is a common enterprise and what are efforts solely of others. This test, however, is limited to determining those instruments not within any other description contained in Section 2 and which conceivably would escape the scope of the section but for this test. Frankfurter's dissent, however, seems to raise a question brushed over by the court: namely, if as a matter of fact the two contracts are separate transactions, could, as a matter of law, the contracts in question be part of § 2? The court seems, inconsistently, to hold yes.

NOTES:

SEC v. KOSCOT INTERPLANETARY, INC.
497 F.2d 473 (5th Cir. 1974).

NATURE OF CASE: Appeal from order denying injunction.

FACT SUMMARY: Company conducted "sales campaign" for beauty products by distributing shares in its enterprise in turn for which purchasers brought in new "sellers" of the products.

CONCISE RULE OF LAW: An investment contract will be found where the efforts of those other than the investor are the essential and significant managerial efforts, which affect the failure or success of the enterprise as a whole.

FACTS: Koscot Interplanetary, Inc. (D) conducted a multilevel operation for selling cosmetics. The three levels consisted of, in ascending order, "beauty advisor"; supervisors; and distributors; the difference between each level being the amount of the investment and the amount of discounts on cosmetics which are sold to the next lowest level at a greater price. In addition, if the investor brought in a new investor he would receive a percentage of the amount paid by the new prospect to Koscot (D). Prospective investors were solicited by investors to attend opportunity meetings where Koscot employees would read from scripts from which they could not deviate. In addition, employees would give the impression of affluence, and would arrange "Go-Tours." If the prospect decided to invest, the sponsoring investor was not required to do any further work. The district court refused to grant an injunction on the ground that the Koscot arrangement did not involve a sale of investment contract.

ISSUE: In order to find an investment contract, must the efforts of those other than the investor be essential and significant to the ultimate failure or success of the enterprise?

HOLDING AND DECISION: (Gewin, J.) Yes. Under the test of Howey, an investment contract has three elements: an investment of money, in a common enterprise, and under the scheme profits are derived solely from the acts of others. Here, money was clearly invested in a common enterprise which is one where the fortunes of an investor are dependent on the efforts and success of those seeking the investment. The third element is the crucial issue as to whether the Howey should be given a literal or functional approach. A literal approach would frustrate the remedial purpose of the Securities Act and would be circumscribed by an investor's modicum of effort. Case law subsequent to Howey has cautioned against a literal approach and the proper test is whether the efforts made by those other than the investor are the essential and significant managerial efforts which effect the failure or success of the enterprise. Applying this test, the role of investors in Koscot are similar to those in the scheme involved in SEC v. Glen Turner Enterprises; the participation of the investor at the meeting was limited to reading from a script, not much time was spent, and closing the sale required no effort at all. Thus, the investors' return was limited to those efforts of promoters, who retained control over managerial operations upon which the profits of the scheme were dependent, and thus clearly would not be a conventional franchising arrangement.

EDITOR'S ANALYSIS: The Koscot case represents an attempt by a lower court to adequately implement the Supreme Court's test in Howey. Here, the issue was what extent and degree of effort is required by the investor so as not to have the enterprise's profits dependent solely on the efforts of others. While the facts here indicate the proper application of the Howey test, the court's own formulated test to determine the third element seems itself difficult to apply and is dependent on the facts of each case. Again, it is a matter of degree as to whether the efforts of others are the significant and essential managerial efforts. No attempt was made by the court to encompass nonmanagerial efforts.

NOTES:

WALS v. FOX HILLS DEVELOPMENT CORPORATION
24 F.3d 1016 (7th Cir. 1994).

NATURE OF CASE: Appeal from a denial of a request to rescind a time-share sale of real estate.

FACT SUMMARY: After the Walses (P) purchased a time-share in a condominium, which they elected to rent out, they brought this action to rescind the sale, contending that their arrangement with Fox Hills (D) converted the sale to an investment contract that Fox Hills (D) should have registered.

CONCISE RULE OF LAW: A pooling of interests between the developer and each individual investor and also among the investors themselves is required to convert a sale of real estate to a sale of an investment contract.

FACTS: The Walses (P) purchased a time-share in a condominium from Fox Hills Development Corporation (D). They then agreed to swap their week, which was in February, for a week in the summer. However, they decided not to occupy the unit in the summer, allowing Fox Hills (D) to rent it out instead. The Walses (P) would receive the rental minus a 30% fee charged by Fox Hills (D). They later sued for rescission of the time-share contract rental, contending that the unusual rental feature of their relationship with Fox Hills (D) converted the sale from a sale of real estate to a sale of an investment contract that Fox Hills (D) was required to register under the Securities Act. The Walses (P) argued that Fox Hills' (D) failure to so register the sale entitled them to a rescission. The district court disagreed. The Walses (P) appealed.

ISSUE: Is a pooling of interests between the developer and each individual investor and also among the investors themselves required to convert a sale of real estate to a sale of an investment contract?

HOLDING AND DECISION: (Posner, J.) Yes. A pooling of interests between the developer and each individual investor and also among the investors themselves is required to convert a sale of real estate to a sale of an investment contract. This requirement is known as "horizontal commonality." Here, there was a pooling of weeks, in a sense, because the Walses (P) selected their summer swap week from a "pool" of available weeks. But there was not a pooling of profits, which is essential to horizontal commonality. A share of stock, for example, is an undivided interest in an enterprise, entitling the owner to a pro rata share in the enterprise's profits. The Walses (P) bought a "temporal slice" of a condo and then rented it. The unusual form of the rental arrangement did not convert the sale of the home into an investment contract. Affirmed.

EDITOR'S ANALYSIS: A number of circuits have allowed rescission under the fact pattern presented in this case. These circuits believe mere "vertical commonality," that is, a division of rental income between the developer and the condominium owner is all that is required to create an investment contract. The Supreme Court has avoided the issue so far.

NOTES:

HOCKING v. DUBOIS
885 F.2d 1449 (9th Cir. 1989), cert. denied, 494 U.S. 1078 (1990).

NATURE OF CASE: Appeal from summary judgment in an action for violation of federal securities law.

FACT SUMMARY: Hocking (P) contended his purchase of a condominium and use of a rental pool arrangement in Hawaii from DuBois (D), a real estate agent, qualified as a security for purposes of the antifraud provisions in the Securities Exchange Act of 1934.

CONCISE RULE OF LAW: A real estate purchase constitutes purchase of a security for purposes of antifraud provisions where the investor has no power of control over the management of a common enterprise.

FACTS: Hocking (P) employed DuBois (D), a real estate agent, to search for a condominium in Hawaii for Hocking (P) to buy. DuBois (D) recommended a resort complex in Honolulu whereby Hocking (P) would participate in a rental pool arrangement (RPA). In a rental pool, rental income from individual units is pooled and then distributed on a pro rata basis to the owners of the units. Hocking (P), concluding that rental income from the RPA would cover the mortgage payments, purchased the condominium. Hotel Corporation of the Pacific (HCP), which operated the RPA, contracted with Hocking (P) to manage his condominium. Hocking (P) had the option to cancel the rental pool arrangement at any time. Hocking (P) defaulted on the property and contended that failure to receive the expected rental income caused the default. Hocking (P) then filed suit under the antifraud provisions of the Securities Exchange Act of 1934. DuBois (D) responded that the transaction was not a security for purposes of the Act. The trial court agreed and granted summary judgment to Dubois (D). Hocking (P) appealed.

ISSUE: May a real estate purchase constitute a security purchase for purposes of antifraud provisions in the Securities Act?

HOLDING AND DECISION: (Goodwin, J.) Yes. A real estate purchase constitutes purchase of a security for purposes of antifraud provisions where the investor has no power of control over the management of a common enterprise. In SEC v. W.J. Howey Co., 328 U.S. 293 (1946), the Supreme Court formulated a test to determine whether a real estate transaction qualifies as a security. Under the Howey test, there must be an investment of money in a common enterprise with an expectation of profits solely from the efforts of others. Although real estate purchases alone lack a pooling of interests, real estate transactions that involve a package of property and an RPA qualify as common enterprises. Hocking (P) asserts that the condominium sale and the RPA were presented as part of one transaction by DuBois (D). Therefore, a genuine issue of fact exists as to whether the transaction was an investment in a common enterprise. Generally, where the investor has control over the property, the profits will not be produced solely by the efforts of others. However, where an unsophisticated and inexperienced investor makes a passive investment that provides no ability for ultimate control, the expectation of profits will be considered to result from the efforts of others. Hocking (P) was not required to enter into the RPA with HCP and had various termination rights. However, since other investors in the condominium were using HCP, it was practically impossible to replace HCP as managing agent. Therefore, Hocking (P) has raised genuine issues of fact regarding whether the transaction should be considered a security. Thus, summary judgment was inappropriate. Reversed and remanded.

DISSENT: (Norris, J.) The majority's test is much too imprecise to serve as a meaningful standard for determining when a realtor's discussion of an available RPA transforms a condominium sale into a security sale.

DISSENT: (Wiggins, J.) The Securities Acts should reach only the rental pool operator's offering of collateral agreements that induce condominium owners to forego personal use and control on the promise of profits to be derived through an enterprise beyond their control.

EDITOR'S ANALYSIS: The court of appeals was split six to five in this case. The dissenting judges noted that the majority decision makes it difficult for real estate agents to know whether they may advise prospective purchasers of rental pooling arrangements without implicating federal securities laws. Furthermore, the majority completely disregarded the SEC's own opinion that its rule did not apply to Hocking's (P) transaction.

NOTES:

UNITED HOUSING FOUNDATION, INC. v. FORMAN
421 U.S. 837 (1975).

NATURE OF CASE: Appeal from denial of motion to dismiss action for violations of federal securities laws.

FACT SUMMARY: United Housing (UHF) (D), the developer of Co-op City, required that prospective purchasers (P) buy shares of stock in order to occupy an apartment in the development.

CONCISE RULE OF LAW: Commercial transactions in stock do not constitute securities under the Securities Acts where the purpose of the transaction is not to invest for profit.

FACTS: The City of New York provides long-term, low-interest loans and tax exemptions to private developers to encourage low-cost cooperative housing. UHF (D), a nonprofit corporation, developed Co-op City, which houses 50,000 people in thirty-five high-rise buildings. UHF (D) organized Riverbay (D) to own and operate Co-op City. To acquire an apartment, a prospective purchaser had to buy eighteen shares of stock in Riverbay (D) for each room desired. The sole purpose of these shares was to enable the purchaser to move in to Co-op City. The shares could not be transferred, had no voting rights, and had to be sold back at their initial selling price when the tenant moved out of Co-op City. During the initial development, UHF (D) sought to attract tenants to partially fund the construction costs. When the costs ran higher than expected, the average monthly rental charges were increased to reflect the cost overruns. Fifty-seven residents (P) of Co-op City filed suit against UHF (D) and Riverbay (D), claiming that the initial offer falsely claimed that the tenants would not be responsible for cost increases in the construction. The residents (P) claimed that the alleged misrepresentations violated federal securities laws. UHF (D) responded that the transactions did not involve securities, and the district court granted a motion to dismiss. The court of appeals reversed, and UHF (D) appealed.

ISSUE: Do commercial transactions involving the sale of stock constitute securities where the purpose is not to invest for profit?

HOLDING AND DECISION: (Powell, J.) No. Commercial transactions do not constitute securities under the Securities Acts where the purpose is not to invest for profit. Simply labeling a transaction a sale of "stock" does not make it a security transaction. The primary purpose of the Securities Acts of 1933 and 1934 was to eliminate abuses in the sales of securities to raise capital for profit-making purposes. Because securities transactions are economic in character, Congress intended the application of these laws to turn on the economic realities underlying the transactions, rather than the name assigned to them. Generally, stocks provide the right to receive dividends contingent upon an apportionment of profits, are negotiable, and confer voting rights. A transaction labeled a stock purchase is not a security transaction unless it involves those three characteristics. Persons who intend to acquire an apartment for personal use are not buying investment securities simply because the transaction is evidenced by something called "stock." Furthermore, a share in Riverside (D) was not an "investment contract" as defined by the Securities Acts. A commercial dealing is not an investment contract unless it involves an investment with an expectation of profits. The residents and shareholders (P) in UHF (D) and Riverbay (D) were not entitled to any profit through their ownership of the stock and intended only to acquire a place to live. Therefore, the transaction does not qualify as a security for purposes of antifraud provisions. Reversed.

EDITOR'S ANALYSIS: The court rejected the contention that the residents (P) of Co-op City could profit on the transaction due to income from leasing of parking spaces and washing machines since such income was too speculative. Housing cooperatives that allow owners to sell their stock for profit are distinguishable from this case. See Grenader v. Spitz, 537 F.2d 612 (2nd Cir. 1976).

NOTES:

INTERNATIONAL BROTHERHOOD OF TEAMSTERS, CHAUFFEURS, WAREHOUSEMEN & HELPERS OF AMERICA v. DANIEL
439 U.S. 551 (1979).

NATURE OF CASE: Action to obtain pension benefits.

FACT SUMMARY: Daniel (P), who was denied pension benefits under the plan adopted by the Teamsters (D), claimed that the plan was a "security" subject to the disclosure rules in the Securities Acts.

CONCISE RULE OF LAW: Noncontributory, compulsory pension plans are not "securities" and therefore are not subject to the various requirements of the Securities Acts.

FACTS: Through collective bargaining, the Teamsters (D) obtained a noncontributory, compulsory pension plan for their members, one of whom was Daniel (D). Basically, Daniel (D) was denied the pension he thought he had coming because his required 20 years of continuous service was interrupted by one five-month layoff and a four-month period where his employer made no contributions for him to the plan because of embezzlement by the employer's bookkeeper. When he brought suit to obtain the benefits he felt he deserved, Daniel (D) argued that the pension plan constituted a "security" and was therefore subject to the various requirements of the Securities Acts. Furthermore, he asserted that those involved in the pension plan had misrepresented and omitted stating material facts with respect to the value of a covered employee's interest in the plan. A motion to dismiss the complaint was denied by the district court, which held that the plan created an "investment contract" and therefore a "security."

ISSUE: Do the Securities Acts encompass as "securities" noncontributory, compulsory pension plans?

HOLDING AND DECISION: (Powell, J.) No. Noncontributory, compulsory pension plans are not considered "securities" as that term is used in the Securities Acts, so they are subject to none of their provisions. Whatever Daniel (D) gave up to participate in the plan, it was a small part of his total employment package; it is an economic fact that employees sell their labor primarily to obtain a livelihood and not to make an investment by way of the attached pension plan. An "investment contract" looks primarily to the managerial or entrepreneurial efforts of others to achieve profits, but the major source of income to this plan and others like it is employer contributions and not investment return. The SEC's contention that this type of plan should be considered a "security" is flatly contradicted by its past actions. Furthermore, passage of a comprehensive package governing pension plans in 1974 (ERISA) indicates Congress felt the area had been left untouched by more general legislation, like the Securities Acts. Reversed.

EDITOR'S ANALYSIS: Daniel (D) would have had a cause of action under the legislation passed in 1974 dealing specifically with pension plans and called ERISA, but it took effect after he retired. It regulates the substantive terms of the plan, sets standards for plan funding, and sets limits on the eligibility requirements an employee must meet.

NOTES:

MARINE BANK v. WEAVER
455 U.S. 551 (1982).

NATURE OF CASE: Appeal from the denial of a motion to dismiss an action for violation of federal securities laws.

FACT SUMMARY: Weaver (P) sought to make fraud claims under federal securities laws after pledging a certificate of deposit from Marine Bank (D) as security to guarantee a loan.

CONCISE RULE OF LAW: A unique certificate of deposit issued by a federally regulated bank does not constitute a security under the antifraud provisions of the federal securities laws.

FACTS: Weaver (P) purchased a $50,000 certificate of deposit from Marine Bank (D) in 1978. The certificate had a six-year maturity and was insured by the Federal Deposit Insurance Corporation. Weaver (P) pledged the certificate of deposit to Marine Bank (D) to guarantee a $65,000 loan made by Marine Bank (D) to Columbus Packing, a slaughterhouse and retail meat market. Columbus agreed to pay Weaver (P) 50% of their net profits, $100 a month, and let Weaver (P) use its barn and pasture. Weaver (P) was also given the right to veto future borrowing by Columbus. Weaver's (P) certificate of deposit was used immediately to pay Columbus' overdue obligations to Marine Bank (D), although Weaver (P) alleged that Marine Bank (D) had told them that Columbus could use the loan as working capital. Columbus went bankrupt shortly thereafter, and Weaver (P) filed suit against Marine Bank (D) for violating §10(b) of the Securities Exchange Act of 1934. The trial court dismissed the action. The court of appeals reversed after concluding that the CD and the separate agreement between Weaver (P) and Columbus might be securities. Marine Bank (D) appealed.

ISSUE: Is a unique certificate of deposit issued by a federally regulated bank a security?

HOLDING AND DECISION: (Burger, C.J.) No. A unique certificate of deposit issued by a federally regulated bank does not constitute a security under the antifraud provisions of the federal securities laws. The Securities Exchange Act of 1934 defines "securities" broadly. The Act was meant to cover all types of instruments in the commercial world that have the attributes of securities. Securities often involve long-term debt obligations. Certificates of deposit are similar to long-term debt obligations held to be securities, except for the fact that certificates issued by federally regulated banks are subject to a comprehensive set of regulations governing the banking industry. Furthermore, securities usually involve a public offering to a number of potential investors. Therefore, private transactions entailing a unique agreement do not fall within the ordinary concept of a security. Weaver (P) purchased a certificate of deposit from a federally regulated bank. Such a certificate is governed by other regulatory schemes created to provide fraud protections. Furthermore, the agreement between Weaver (P) and Columbus was a unique agreement, negotiated one-on-one by the parties, which was not designed to be traded publicly. Therefore, it does not qualify as a security transaction either. Reversed.

EDITOR'S ANALYSIS: This case represents yet another example of an attempt to limit the expanding definition of securities initiated by the landmark case of SEC v. W.J. Howey Co., 328 U.S. 293 (1946). Although the Court mentions Howey, its decision effectively repudiates the Howey common enterprise test. From a policy standpoint, public offerings are distinguishable from private agreements because dissemination of information requirements for securities can be justified by economies of scale for public sales.

NOTES:

LANDRETH TIMBER CO. v. LANDRETH
471 U.S. 681 (1985).

NATURE OF CASE: Appeal from dismissal of action for rescission and damages.

FACT SUMMARY: Landreth Timber Company (P) purchased all the stock in a timber mill from Landreth (D) and sued under the securities laws.

CONCISE RULE OF LAW: A sale of shares of stock will be covered by the securities laws, irrespective of the nature of the stockholder's role in managing the corporation.

FACTS: The Landreths (D) offered to sell the stock of their lumber business. Dennis and Bolten became interested and formed Landreth Timber Co. (P), which acquired 100% of the stock of the lumber company. Landreth (D) was retained as a consultant. The offering of stock was of an interstate nature and was not registered per the 1933 Securities Act. The business did not do as well as anticipated, and Landreth Timber Company (P) filed a suit under securities laws seeking rescission and damages. The district court held the transaction to be the sale of a business rather than securities, and the court of appeals affirmed.

ISSUE: Will a sale of shares of stock be covered by the securities laws, irrespective of the stockholder's role in managing the corporation?

HOLDING AND DECISION: (Powell, J.) Yes. A sale of shares of stock will be covered by the securities laws, irrespective of the nature of the stockholder's role in managing the corporation. Section 2(1) of the 1933 Act clearly defines a security as "any ... stock." It does not make distinctions based on the role of the purchaser in managing the corporation. The Court, in SEC v. W. J. Howey Co., 328 U.S. 293 at 299, defined a security in terms of a passive investment without managerial control. In that case, however, it was the sale of an unusual investment not easily recognizable as a security that was at issue. The Court's Howey test only applies to such unusual investments. Stock, on the other hand, is the investment that most readily comes to mind when one mentions "security," and this fact, coupled with the clear statutory language, necessitates the holding that all stock sales are covered by securities laws. Reversed.

DISSENT: (Stevens, J.) Congress only meant the 1933 and 1934 Securities Acts to apply to publicly-held sales.

EDITOR'S ANALYSIS: Wherever somebody sues based on securities laws, an attempt is almost always made to come under federal securities laws. Procedural advantages often exist in federal court. More importantly, if a violation of the 1933 Act is found, the plaintiff is absolutely entitled to rescission, without having to prove damages.

NOTES:

KOCH v. HANKINS
928 F.2d 1471 (9th Cir. 1991).

NATURE OF CASE: Appeal from dismissal of action seeking damages for securities laws violations.

FACT SUMMARY: A group of investors (P) in general partnerships formed to buy land to grow jojoba brought an action under federal securities laws against the promoters (D) of the partnerships.

CONCISE RULE OF LAW: Interests in general partnerships may be classified as securities when investors are prevented from exercising meaningful control over their investment.

FACTS: A group of 160 investors (P) including Koch (P), primarily urban professionals, invested in a series of thirty-five general partnerships created to grow jojoba beans on a 2700-acre plantation. Each partnership was responsible for a designated 80 acres; however, the management and cultivation of the plantation treated the 2700 acres as one unit. The partnership agreements gave the investors (P) some opportunity to actively manage their parcels. As a practical matter, no investor (P) had any experience in agriculture, and only by ousting the plantation's management (a practical impossibility) could the investors effect serious change in how the plantation was run. The investment proved unprofitable, and a class of investors (P) sued for securities laws violations. The district court dismissed, holding that interests in general partnerships were not securities. An appeal was taken.

ISSUE: May interests in general partnerships be classified as securities?

HOLDING AND DECISION: (Fletcher, J.) Yes. Interests in general partnerships may be classified as securities where the investors are prevented from exercising meaningful control over investment. A "security" is defined as an investment in a common enterprise managed by others. In other words, a security is a "passive" investment. Since, by definition, a general partner in a general partnership has managerial authority, the district court held that the interests at issue here were not securities. However, in deciding whether an investment is a security, a court is not limited to the express terms of an investment agreement but may look to its function. If an agreement leaves so little power in the hands of the investor that he is a de facto limited partner, his interest may be a security. His interest may also be a security if the investor is so inexperienced as to make exercise of his powers impractical or if the venturer is dependent on the managerial skill of others. In this case, while the investors were called general partners, a triable issue exists as to whether one or more of the above situations exists, leading to securities laws jurisdiction. The district court's grant of summary judgment was therefore improper. Reversed.

EDITOR'S ANALYSIS: An interest in a limited partnership is, by definition, a passive investment for the limited partner. General partnerships are more problematic for purposes of securities law jurisdiction. On paper, general partners are not passive investors. There is a split among the circuits as to how far beyond the partnership agreement inquiry should go.

NOTES:

REVES v. ERNST & YOUNG
494 U.S. 56 (1990).

NATURE OF CASE: Appeal from an award of damages in action for fraud under federal securities laws.

FACT SUMMARY: Investors (P) in demand notes issued by the Farmer's Cooperative brought suit against Ernst & Young (D), who prepared the financial statements under federal securities laws.

CONCISE RULE OF LAW: Promissory notes with immediate maturity qualify as securities when they are offered and sold to members of the public who seek to invest for profit.

FACTS: The Farmer's Cooperative of Arkansas and Oklahoma sold promissory notes payable on demand by the holder in order to support its general business operations. The notes were uninsured and paid a variable rate of interest that was adjusted according to the rate paid by local financial institutions. The Cooperative marketed the sale of the demand notes through general advertising. In 1984, the Cooperative filed for bankruptcy while 1,600 investors (P) held demand notes worth $10 million. A class of investors (P) filed suit against Ernst & Young (D), the accounting firm who had audited the Cooperative, for violations of the antifraud provisions of the Securities Exchange Act of 1934. At trial, the note holders (P) received a $6.1 million judgment, and Ernst & Young (D) appealed, contending that the demand notes were not covered by federal securities laws.

ISSUE: May demand notes qualify as securities?

HOLDING AND DECISION: (Marshall, J.) Yes. Promissory notes with immediate maturity qualify as securities when they are offered and sold to the members of the public who seek to invest for profit. The Securities Exchange Act of 1934 sought to broadly define securities to encompass virtually any instrument that is sold as an investment. The intent of Congress was to regulate security investment regardless of its form. The family resemblance test provides the best framework for determining whether an instrument is a security investment. Under the family resemblance test, every note is initially presumed to be a security. However, this presumption may be rebutted by showing four factors. First, the motivations of the seller and the buyer are assessed. If the seller's purpose is to raise money for a business, and the buyer is primarily interested in profit, the note is likely to be a security. Secondly, the plan of distribution is examined. Public offerings are likely to be securities. Thirdly, the expectations of the investing public is considered. Finally, the existence of another regulatory scheme reducing the risk of the investment is factored into the determination. Here, the Cooperative sold the demand notes to raise money for its business, and the purchasers expected to earn a profit in the form of interest. The demand notes were advertised publicly and were characterized as investments. Therefore, the public could reasonably expect them to be treated as securities. Finally, the demand notes offered by the Cooperative were uninsured and not covered by any other regulatory scheme. Thus, applying the family resemblance test, the demand notes sold by the Cooperative are similar to security investments and thus are covered by federal securities law. Moreover, the fact that the demand notes had an immediate maturity does not qualify them for the exemption for short-term notes provided by §3(a)(10) because Congress intended that investments of all descriptions be regulated to prevent fraud and abuse. Affirmed.

CONCURRENCE: (Stevens, J.) The legislative history of § 3(a)(10) indicates that the exclusion for short-term notes applies only to commercial paper, not to notes.

DISSENT: (Rehnquist, C.J.) The specific language of § 3(a)(10) excludes from the scope of federal securities law notes with immediate maturity. According to state law, the demand notes issued by the Cooperative matured on the date they were sold since they could be redeemed immediately. Therefore, they are expressly exempted.

EDITOR'S ANALYSIS: Many commentators believe that the family resemblance test articulated by the majority is essentially a restatement of the test in SEC v. W.J. Howey Co., 328 U.S. 293 (1946). Even though the same factors are present in both tests, the Howey test was explicitly rejected by the majority as irrelevant. See Gordon, Interplanetary Intelligence About Promissory Notes as Securities, 69 Tex. L. Rev. 383 (1990).

NOTES:

BANCO ESPANOL DE CREDITO v. SECURITY PACIFIC NAT'L BANK
973 F.2d 51 (2d Cir. 1992), cert. denied, 509 U.S. 903 (1993).

NATURE OF CASE: Appeal from dismissal of action alleging securities violations and seeking rescission of loan note purchase.

FACT SUMMARY: Investor Banco Espanol (P) contended it had purchased loan notes from Security Pacific (D) in a series of investment transactions that it termed "securities."

CONCISE RULE OF LAW: Loan participations, i.e., the practice of selling loans to other institutions, are not "securities."

FACTS: As a primary lender, Security Pacific (D) made a series of short-term loans to Integrated. In an attempt to diversify its risk, Security Pacific (D) subsequently sold participations in these loans to various institutional lenders, including Banco Espanol (P). Security Pacific (D) assumed no responsibility for the ability of Integrated to repay its loan. Integrated eventually went bankrupt and defaulted on the loans. Banco Espanol (P) filed suit against Security Pacific (D) to rescind its purchase of the participation, contending that Security Pacific (D) had not disclosed Integrated's true financial condition in violation of § 12(2) of the 1933 Securities Act. The district court dismissed the suit on the grounds that loan participations of the sort sold by Security Pacific (D) were not "securities" under the Act. Banco Espanol (P) appealed.

ISSUE: Are loan participations, i.e., the practice of selling loans to other institutions, "securities?"

HOLDING AND DECISION: (Altimari, J.) No. Loan participations, i.e., the practice of selling loans to other institutions, are not "securities." Clearly, traditional loans by commercial banks to their customers for use in the customers' current operations are not securities. However, to determine whether or not participation in such loans would constitute "securities," the following four factors, set forth in Reves v. Ernst & Young, 494 U.S. 46 (1990). must be applied: (1) the motivations behind the transaction; (2) the plan of distribution of the instrument; (3) the reasonable expectations of the investing public; and (4) whether another regulatory scheme renders the application of the securities laws unnecessary. In this case, Security Pacific (D) was motivated by a desire to diversify its risk, and Banco Espanol (P) was motivated by a need for a short-term return on excess cash. Therefore the overall motivation was the promotion of commercial purposes, not the sort of investment in a business enterprise more likely to be called a security. Secondly, the plan of distribution was to sophisticated financial institutions and not to the general public. Thirdly, the sophisticated purchasers knew they were engaging in loan participations, not investments. Finally, a separate regulatory body, the Office of the Comptroller of the Currency, has issued specific guidelines regarding the sale of loan participations. Therefore, these four factors, taken together, show that loan participations in this case do not satisfy the statutory definition of "notes" which are "securities." Affirmed.

DISSENT: (Oakes, J.) The majority has misread the facts. Security Pacific's (D) so-called loan participation program involved hundreds of purchasers, who were solicited by Security Pacific's corporate debt — not commercial loan — department on a daily basis, and who were offered a range of investment options. In an effort to compete with the commercial paper market, Security Pacific promoted the liquidity of its debt instruments, which were unsecured notes with short-term maturities. Moreover, Security Pacific provided investors with very limited information about the actual borrowers, whereas in genuine loan participations, participants negotiate one-on-one with the lead lender with full credit disclosure. Regardless of the majority's characterization, these loan notes were purchased by Banco Espanol (P) in investment transactions and, accordingly, are securities.

EDITOR'S ANALYSIS: In this case, Banco Espanol (P) was unable to buck a long tradition of denying banks access to securities laws in their attempts to recoup bad loans. During a lending transaction, banks are assumed to occupy a superior bargaining position and to have access to the sort of disclosures that would make protection under the securities acts superfluous. Of course, as the dissent pointed out, Banco Espanol (P), though sophisticated, was denied the sort of information that would have been available in a typical loan transaction.

NOTES:

CHAPTER 4
THE PUBLIC OFFERING

QUICK REFERENCE RULES OF LAW

1. **Methods of Underwriting.** Securities may be sold through "firm commitment" underwriting whereby a managing underwriter apportions the sale of stock to investment banking firms who resell to the public. (In re National Association of Securities Dealers, Inc.)

2. **To Whom Are the '33 Act's Disclosure Requirements Directed?** Proper disclosure to investors must include a clearly written narrative statement outlining the major aspects of the offering as well as detailed financial information. (Feit v. Leasco Data Processing Equipment Co.)

3. **The Post-Effective Period Problems.** The registrant is subject to the duty to disclose material developments occurring after the effective date of registration if those developments make the registration materially misleading. (SEC v. Manor Nursing Centers, Inc.)

IN RE NATIONAL ASSOCIATION OF SECURITIES DEALERS, INC.
Exchange Act Release No. 17,371 (Dec. 12, 1980).

NATURE OF CASE: Hearing on the fixed-price underwriting system.

FACT SUMMARY: The SEC explained the scope of the activities of managing underwriters in "firm commitment" sales of securities.

CONCISE RULE OF LAW: Securities may be sold through "firm commitment" underwriting whereby a managing underwriter apportions the sale of stock to investment banking firms who resell to the public.

FACTS: Section 5 of the Securities Act makes demands on those involved in distributing a security. Section 5 bars any offers to sell and sales of a security until a registration statement has become effective. The intended purpose of the registration is to provide information to discourage fraudulent promotion. A prospectus must accompany any written offers to sell registered securities. Section 11 of the Securities Act imposes liability on the issuer of stock for any material omissions in registration statements. Public offerings of stock typically occur through underwriters. Underwriters, or investment bankers, are often faced with conflicts of interest. The SEC held hearings on the role of underwriters in public offerings of securities.

ISSUE: May securities be sold through "firm commitment" underwriting by investment banking firms who receive a commission on resale to the public?

HOLDING AND DECISION: Yes. Securities may be sold through "firm commitment" underwriting whereby a managing underwriter apportions the sale of stock to investment banking firms who resell to the public. Corporations are able to raise money in different ways. They may sell securities through public or private offerings. In a public offering, companies often use brokers to sell the securities. This is accomplished through "firm commitment," or "best efforts," underwriting. In best efforts underwriting, the broker is paid a fee by the corporation for selling the security on behalf of the issuer at the offering price. In firm commitment underwriting, the investment banking firms purchase the securities and then resell them to the public. Usually, investment banking firms organize an underwriting syndicate controlled by a manager who executes the agreement. The managing underwriter apportions the securities to the brokers who are part of the agreement. The difference between public offering price and the amount received by the issuer is known as the "gross spread," which represents: (1) the managing underwriter's fee; (2) the underwriting compensation; and (3) the seller's concession. The investment banking firms each underwrite a portion of the whole amount, but usually each broker can draw as much from the syndicate as they are able to sell to the public. The managing underwriter determines the allocations.

EDITOR'S ANALYSIS: The managing underwriter usually prepares the issuer and gives advice far in advance of the actual offering. The managing underwriter may tell the issuer the amount that should be sold and the best time to offer the security. The underwriter may also assist in the preparation of the registration statements required by the SEC.

NOTES:

FEIT v. LEASCO DATA PROCESSING EQUIPMENT CORP.
332 F. Supp. 544 (E.D.N.Y. 1971).

NATURE OF CASE: Class action for damages for misrepresentations in registration statements in a securities offering.

FACT SUMMARY: Feit (P) filed a class action on behalf of investors who exchanged Reliance Insurance stock for Leasco (D) stock in a public offering, based on information in the registration statement.

CONCISE RULE OF LAW: Proper disclosure to investors must include a clearly written narrative statement outlining the major aspects of the offering as well as detailed financial information.

FACTS: Feit (P) and other shareholders in Reliance Insurance exchanged their stock for preferred shares in Leasco (D). Feit (P) filed a class action suit alleging damages resulting from alleged misrepresentations and omissions in the registration statement prepared in conjunction with the offering. The Securities Act of 1933 requires full disclosure in the registration statements.

ISSUE: Must proper disclosure to investors include both a narrative statement and detailed financial information?

HOLDING AND DECISION: (Weinstein, J.) Yes. Proper disclosure to investors must include a clearly written narrative statement outlining the major aspects of the offering as well as detailed financial information. The keystone of the Securities Act of 1933 is the accurate disclosure of information. Investors need complete, accurate, and intelligible information about a company in order to make intelligent investment decisions regarding securities offered for sale. This information requirement assures the integrity of the free market and promotes good general business practices. Under the Securities Act, disclosure must not only be in compliance technically but also must be effective in conveying information. Therefore, prospectuses must be clearly understandable and comprehensible to the public. Companies must not disguise critical information within a morass of useless financial data. Companies must strike a pragmatic balance between the needs of unsophisticated investors and knowledgeable insiders. Thus, a clearly written narrative statement which outlines the major aspects of the offering is required, along with detailed financial information that will have meaning only to experts. The objective of full disclosure under the Act can only be achieved through the inclusion of both the outline and the details. [The application and holding has been edited out of the decision — there is no mention of the resolution of the case.]

EDITOR'S ANALYSIS: Some commentators believe that investors do not get their information directly from the prospectus in the registration statements. They believe that nearly all businesses use technical descriptions that are only useful and familiar to professionals in the field. Therefore, nearly all investors actually get their information filtered through the opinion of experts. See Kripke, The SEC, the Accountants, Some Myths and Some Realities, 45 N.Y.U.L. Rev. 1151 (1970).

NOTES:

SEC v. MANOR NURSING CENTERS, INC.
458 F.2d 1082 (2d Cir. 1972).

NATURE OF CASE: Action for disgorgement of profits and income, injunction, and appointment of trustee to reimburse public investors.

FACT SUMMARY: Manor (D) conducted an offering of 450,000 shares on an all or nothing basis. Funds were to be held in escrow and not used until all terms of the offering were met. All shares were not sold, Manor (D) knew of this but did not return the funds to the investors according to the terms of the offering.

CONCISE RULE OF LAW: The registrant is subject to the duty to disclose material developments occurring after the effective date of registration if those developments make the registration materially misleading.

FACTS: Manor Nursing Centers Inc. (D) conducted a primary and secondary offering of 450,000 shares to be offered and sold on an all or nothing basis, i.e., if all shares were not sold within 60 days the offering would terminate and all funds would be returned with interest. Funds were to be held in escrow, unavailable for other use until terms of the offering were met. Manor (D) and selling stockholders had not sold all shares within the 60-day period and had not received all the proceeds expected. Manor (D) and selling stockholders knew or should have known that the preconditions for retaining the proceeds had not been met but the funds were not refunded to the public investors. The SEC (P) brought suit alleging violations of the antifraud provisions of the 1933 Act, §§ 17(a) and 10(b) of the 1934 Act contending that Manor (D) should have disclosed that all shares were not sold, that an escrow account was not opened, that the funds were not returned to the investors, that shares were sold for other than cash, and that certain individuals received extra compensation for agreeing to participate in the sale.

ISSUE: Is there a duty on a registrant to disclose developments occurring after the effective date of registration which make the previous disclosures materially misleading?

HOLDING AND DECISION: (Timbers, J.) Yes. Although it is not necessary to amend the registration statement, the prospectus must be amended when post effective developments occur which make the previous information false and misleading. A prospectus does not meet the requirements of § 10(a) if information required to be disclosed is materially false and misleading. Manor (D) and selling stockholders violated § 5(b)(2) by delivering Manor securities for sale accompanied by a prospectus which failed to meet § 10(a) requirements since it contained materially false and misleading statements. To meet the requirements of § 10 a prospectus must contain, with certain exceptions, all information contained in the registration statement which must set forth information specified in Schedule A. Schedule A requires inclusion of the following items, among others: 1) the use of the proceeds, 2) estimated net profits, 3) price of the public offering, 4) any variation from that price, 5) all commissions or discounts paid to underwriters, directly or indirectly. Since Manor (D) failed to inform the public that some shares were issued for consideration other than cash and that some individuals received extra compensation for agreeing to participate in the offering, the prospectus failed to set forth Schedule A information making it misleading. Manor (D) was also obligated to inform the investing public that the issue was not fully subscribed, that the funds were not returned, that the escrow account was not opened. The fact that these developments occurred after the effective date of registration is immaterial even though the SEC has held that the registration statement need not be amended for post effective changes. These decisions have held that the prospectus must be amended to reflect such changes. Moreover, the misappropriation of the proceeds of the sale constituted a fraud on public investors in violation of § 17(a) of the 1933 Act. Manor (D) also violated Rule 10b-9 since they represented that the securities were offered and sold on an "all or nothing" basis and did not fulfill the requirements of the Rule. Rule 10b-9 requires that a security offered or sold on an "all or nothing" basis must be part of a distribution made on condition that all or a specific amount of a consideration paid will be returned if all securities offered are not sold at a specified price within a specified time and that the total amount due the seller is not received by him by a specified date. Judgment affirmed except as to disgorgement of profits and income; as to this, reversed and remanded.

EDITOR'S ANALYSIS: This case illustrates the obligation placed upon issuers of stock to update material to prevent misleading the public investors. Even though the material was accurate at the time of filing, subsequent events may make it misleading and the issuer is obligated to supplement the prospectus although there is no obligation to amend the registration statement. Correction of the prospectus may be made by placing a sticker on the cover and supplementing the information or preparing a revised prospectus. Although the revisions need not be processed by the SEC, copies of the supplemental prospectus must be filed with the SEC as soon as its first use.

NOTES:

CHAPTER 5
EXEMPT TRANSACTIONS

QUICK REFERENCE RULES OF LAW

1. **Judicial Guidelines.** In order for the sale of intrastate securities to be exempt from federal laws, the predominant amount of income-producing activity must be conducted within the state. (Busch v. Carpenter)

2. **Mapping the Scope of the Exemption.** The exemption in § 4(1) of the Securities Act of 1933, which exempts transactions by an issuer not involving any public offering from the registration requirement, applies only when all the offerees have access to the same kind of information that the Act would make available if registration were required. (SEC v. Ralston Purina Co.)

3. **Offeree Qualification: Sophistication and Access to Information.** That an investor is sophisticated is not in itself sufficient to exempt an offering from registration requirements. (Doran v. Petroleum Management Corp.)

4. **The Sophistication Standard of Rule 506.** For an issuer to rely on the safe harbor provisions of Rule 506, Regulation D, it must reasonably believe that nonaccredited investors meet sophistication standards. (Mark v. FSC Securities Corp.)

5. **Limitation on the Manner and Scope of an Offering.** When a broker-dealer advertises an offering, the targets of any solicitation or advertisement must have a pre-existing relationship with the offeror. (In the Matter of Kenman Corp.)

BUSCH v. CARPENTER
827 F.2d 653 (10th Cir. 1987).

NATURE OF CASE: Appeal from the dismissal of action to rescind stock purchases.

FACT SUMMARY: Sonic (D) sold stock in an intrastate offering to Utah residents and then merged with an Illinois corporation, leaving Sonic (D) with assets mainly in Illinois.

CONCISE RULE OF LAW: In order for the sale of intrastate securities to be exempt from federal laws, the predominant amount of income-producing activity must be conducted within the state.

FACTS: Sonic (D), a Utah corporation, raised $500,000 through an intrastate stock offering to state residents in 1980. Sonic had no prior operating history but maintained its office and records in Utah. In 1981, Carpenter (D), the president of Sonic (D), was approached by Mason, an oil and gas promoter from Illinois, about a merger of operations. A merger agreement was reached whereby a controlling block of stock in Sonic (D) was issued to Mason, who transferred an Illinois drilling company that he owned to Sonic (D). Mason then transferred the bulk of the proceeds from the intrastate stock offering to an Illinois bank. In other words, most of the proceeds of Sonic's (D) intrastate offering ended up in Illinois. Busch (P) and other investors purchased stock in 1981 after the merger and subsequently sought to rescind the purchase through application of federal securities laws. Sonic (D) and Carpenter (D) responded that the sale of the securities was exempt from federal laws because it was an intrastate distribution. The district court dismissed the action, and Busch (P) appealed.

ISSUE: Is the sale of intrastate securities exempt from federal laws where the predominant amount of income-producing activity by the company is conducted outside the state?

HOLDING AND DECISION: (Seymour, J.) No. In order for the sale of intrastate securities to be exempt from federal laws, the predominant amount of income-producing activity must be conducted within the state. The Securities Act of 1933 applies to all sales of securities. However, an exemption is provided when initial sales are only to state residents. The exemption is not applicable if the stock is sold to purchasers who intend to resell it out of state. A corporation makes a prima facie case for the exemption upon proof that the initial sales were only to residents of the state. The party challenging the exemption then has the burden of proving that the securities had not come to rest within the state before resale. In this case, Carpenter (D) did not know Mason until after the initial public offering. Therefore, there is no evidence that original buyers sought to evade federal securities law. The intrastate exemption is also inapplicable when the company is not doing business within the state. The doing business requirement is satisfied when the issue is conducting a predominant amount of the income-producing activity within its home state. Thus, an issuer is not entitled to the exemption merely by opening an office in a particular state. Sonic (D) only has an office in Utah and transferred virtually all of its assets to Mason in Illinois. Furthermore, there is no evidence that Sonic (D) made any effort to find investing opportunities in Utah. Therefore, there is a genuine issue of fact regarding the intention of Sonic (D) to comply with intrastate offering exemption. This precludes summary judgment. Reversed.

EDITOR'S ANALYSIS: Rule 147 provides a safe harbor holding period of nine months for the intrastate exemption. In other words, a bright-line rule is applied where intrastate security transactions are held for nine months within the state. Sonic (D) merged with Mason after only seven months. Therefore, Rule 147 did not apply.

NOTES:

SEC v. RALSTON PURINA CO.
346 U.S. 119 (1953).

NATURE OF CASE: Action to enjoin the unregistered offerings of stock under the Securities Act of 1933.

FACT SUMMARY: Ralston Purina (D) offered treasury stock to their key employees which the SEC (P) attempted to enjoin.

CONCISE RULE OF LAW: The exemption in § 4(1) of the Securities Act of 1933, which exempts transactions by an issuer not involving any public offering from the registration requirement, applies only when all the offerees have access to the same kind of information that the Act would make available if registration were required.

FACTS: Since 1911, Ralston Purina (D) has had a policy of encouraging stock ownership among its employees and, since 1942, has made unissued common shares available to some of them. Ralston Purina (D) had sold nearly $2,000,000 of stock to employees between the years of 1947 and 1951. They had attempted to avoid the registration requirements of the Securities Act of 1933, under the exemption contained in § 4(1) of the Act which exempted transactions by an issuer not involving any public offering. Each year between 1947 and 1951, Ralston Purina (D) authorized the sale of common stock to employees who, without any solicitation by the Company or its officers or employees, inquired as to how to purchase common stock of Ralston Purina (D). The branch and store managers were advised that only the employees who took the initiative and were interested in buying stock at the present market prices would be able to purchase the stock. Among those taking advantage of the offer were employees with the duties of artist, bakeshop foreman, chow-loading foreman, clerical assistant, copywriter, electrician, stock clerk, mill office clerk, order credit trainee, production trainee, stenographer, and veterinarian. The buyers resided in fifty widely separated communities scattered throughout the United States. The record shows that in 1947, 243 employees bought stock, 20 in 1948, 414 in 1949, 411 in 1950, and, in 1951, 165 made applications to purchase the stock. No actual records were kept showing how many employees were offered the stock, but it is estimated that, in 1951, at least 500 employees were offered the stock. Ralston Purina (D) had approximately 7,000 employees during the years in question. Ralston Purina (D) bases its exemption claim on the classification that all the offerees were key employees in its organization. Its position at trial was that a key employee included an individual who is eligible for promotion; an individual who especially influences others or who advises others; a person whom the employees look to in some special way; one who carries some special responsibility and who is sympathetic to management and one who is ambitious and who the management feels is likely to be promoted to a greater responsibility. They admit, however, that an offering to all of its employees would be a public offering. The district court held that the exemption applied and dismissed the suit and the court of appeals affirmed the decision.

ISSUE: Does an offer of stock by a company to a limited number of its employees automatically qualify for the exemption for transactions not involving any public offering?

HOLDING AND DECISION: (Clark, J.) No. The Securities Act does not define what is a private offering and what is a public offering. It is clear that an offer need not be open to the whole world to qualify as a public offering. If Ralston Purina (D) had made the stock offer to all of its employees, it would have been a public offering. The court looked at the intent of the Securities Act, which is to protect investors by promoting full disclosure of information thought to be necessary for informed investment decisions. When the Act grants an exemption, the class of people involved were not considered as needing the disclosure that the Act normally requires. Therefore, when an offering is made to people who can fend for themselves, the transaction is considered to be one not involving a public offering. Most of the employees purchasing the stock from Ralston Purina (D) were not in a position to know or have access to the kind of information which registration under the Act would disclose, and, therefore, were in need of the protection of the Act. Stock offers made to employees may qualify for the exemption if the employees are executive personnel who, because of their position, have access to the same kind of information that the Act would make available in the form of a registration statement. Absent such a showing of special circumstances, employees are just as much members of the investing public as any of their neighbors in the community. The burden of proof is on the issuer of the stock, who is claiming an exemption to show that he qualifies for the exemption. Also, since the right to an exemption depends on the knowledge of the offerees, the issuer's motives are irrelevant. It didn't matter that Ralston Purina's (D) motives may have been good, because they didn't show that their employees had the requisite information. Therefore, judgment reversed.

EDITOR'S ANALYSIS: The exemption discussed above is now found in § 4(2) instead of § 4(1). This case is considered to be the leading case in this area. The test established in this case is still used in determining whether an offering qualifies for the nonpublic offering exemption of § 4(2). Some of the factors used in determining whether the offerees have sufficient access to information concerning the stock is the number of offerees, the size of the offering, the relationship of the offerees, the manner of the solicitation of the offerees, and the amount of investment experience of the offerees.

DORAN v. PETROLEUM MANAGEMENT CORP.
545 F.2d 893 (5th Cir. 1977).

NATURE OF CASE: Appeal from order dismissing action seeking damages and rescission.

FACT SUMMARY: Petroleum Management (D) contended that an offering purchased by Doran (P) was exempt from registration because Doran (P) was a sophisticated investor.

CONCISE RULE OF LAW: That an investor is sophisticated is not in itself sufficient to exempt an offering from registration requirements.

FACTS: Doran (P) purchased an interest in an oil-and-gas limited partnership. His purchase included assumption of a partnership debt. The partnership proved unsuccessful, and its creditors obtained judgments against it for which Doran (P) became personally liable. He filed an action against the organizer of the partnership, Petroleum Management (D), seeking damages and rescission based on nonregistration of the offering. The district court dismissed, holding that Doran's (P) status as a sophisticated investor nullified the registration requirement. Doran (P) appealed.

ISSUE: Is an investor's sophistication in itself sufficient to exempt an offering from registration requirements?

HOLDING AND DECISION: (Goldberg, J.) No. That an investor is sophisticated is not in itself sufficient to exempt an offering from registration requirements. Also crucial in the exemption analysis is the information available to the offeree. The most sophisticated investor cannot make an intelligent decision absent such information. Consequently, the offeree must either be given, or have access to, information sufficient to make an intelligent decision. The extent to which information must be actually disclosed, as opposed to made available, depends on how close the issuer is to the offeree; the more insider access an offeree has, the less actual disclosure is needed. Here, the district court did not address whether the offeree had a realistic opportunity to learn facts essential to an investment judgment, so a remand is necessary. Reversed.

EDITOR'S ANALYSIS: In this particular case, there were eight offerees, all sophisticated. The number of offerees is relevant in the exemption analysis, along with the size and manner of the offering, and the offeree's sophistication. The more offerees there are, the more likely the offering will be termed a public, not private, offering, and the less likely that a § 4(2) exemption will be available.

NOTES:

MARK v. FSC SECURITIES CORP.
870 F.2d 331 (6th Cir. 1989).

NATURE OF CASE: Action seeking to rescind stock purchases.

FACT SUMMARY: FSC Securities (D), in a stock offering, relied on investors' own conclusions regarding their status as sophisticated investors.

CONCISE RULE OF LAW: For an issuer to rely on the safe harbor provisions of Rule 506, Regulation D, it must reasonably believe that nonaccredited investors meet sophistication standards.

FACTS: FSC Securities Corp. (D) acted as broker-dealer on an issuance of an investment dealing with Spanish Arabian horses. In contacting potential investors, the paperwork contained language to the effect that only sophisticated investors should invest, and the subscription agreements contained a prequalifying questionnaire and required investors to warrant that they had sufficient knowledge to evaluate the investments. These affirmations were accepted by FSC (D) without anyone actually reviewing them. When the investment proved unprofitable, numerous investors (P) sued for rescission due to lack of registration. FSC (D) raised the private placement safe harbor exception of Regulation D, Rule 506, contending that the purchases (P) were sophisticated.

ISSUE: For an issuer to rely on the safe harbor provisions of Rule 506, Regulation D, must it reasonably believe that nonaccredited investors meet sophistication standards?

HOLDING AND DECISION: (Simpson, J.) Yes. For an issuer to rely on the safe harbor provisions of Rule 506, Regulation D, it must reasonably believe that nonaccredited investors meet sophistication standards. This requires that the issuer have undertaken some effort to discover the investors' levels of sophistication. To merely rely on the investors' own assertions in this regard may be sufficient. However, in this case, FSC (D) presented no testimony or evidence other than blank subscription documents that anyone at FSC (D) or the general partnership had actually seen or reviewed the documents executed by the investors (P). Therefore, FSC (D) has not satisfied the burden of proof imposed by Rule 506, that is, the issuer's reasonable belief as to the sophisticated nature of each purchaser (P).

EDITOR'S ANALYSIS: The policy behind the sophisticated investor exemption of Rule 506 has not gone unquestioned. Some have argued that the Rule negates disclosure requirements to those most likely to rely on such disclosures. Such matters notwithstanding, the sophisticated investor exception is firmly rooted in securities law.

NOTES:

IN THE MATTER OF KENMAN CORP.
S.E.C., Fed. Sec. L. Rep. (CCH) ¶ 83,767 (Apr. 19, 1985).

NATURE OF CASE: Administrative proceedings for violations of solicitation rules.

FACT SUMMARY: Kenman Securities (D) advertised an offering to individuals with no prior relationship with Kenman (D).

CONCISE RULE OF LAW: When a broker-dealer advertises an offering, the targets of any solicitation or advertisement must have a pre-existing relationship with the offeror.

FACTS: Kenman Securities (D), a broker-dealer, participated in limited partnership offerings. Information, including a cover letter and a four-page promotional document, was mailed to a list of persons. Included were persons who had participated in prior offerings by Kenman (D). But the list also included "Fortune 500" executives, persons with a history of real estate investment, physicians in California, managerial engineers employed by Hughes Aircraft, and the presidents of certain companies in New Jersey. The SEC (P) instituted proceedings against Kenman (D) and its parent company (D), the general partner, for violations of Rule 502(c), which prohibits the general solicitation of securities.

ISSUE: If a broker-dealer advertises an offering, must the targets of any solicitation or advertisement have a pre-existing relationship with the offeror?

HOLDING AND DECISION: (No judge named) Yes. When a broker-dealer advertises an offering, the targets of any solicitation or advertisement must have a preexisting relationship with the offeror. Rule 502(c) precludes an issuer or any person acting on its behalf, such as a broker-dealer, from offering to sell securities by any form of general solicitation or advertisement. An exception exists for solicitations sent to individuals with a preexisting relationship with the broker-dealer. In this case, only one of the six sources of persons solicited had a prior relationship with Kenman (D). While the persons solicited were likely to have investment experience, that is insufficient to satisfy Rule 502(c).

EDITOR'S ANALYSIS: The requirement of a preexisting relationship is intended in part to allow the issuer to have information about the suitability of the offeree. That is, the issuer must make certain that everyone to which the investment is presented is suitable, not merely those who finally purchase. While this requirement seems unnecessarily strict, the SEC was forced by prior case law and statutory language to draft its safe harbor provision in this manner.

NOTES:

CHAPTER 6
SECONDARY DISTRIBUTIONS

QUICK REFERENCE RULES OF LAW

1. **The Underwriter Concept and Sales for an Issuer.** Foreign bonds must be registered. A party is an underwriter even if he is not authorized by the issuer and even if he does not receive compensation. (SEC v. Chinese Consolidated Benevolent Association)

2. **Control Person Distributions.** Controlling shareholders who utilize brokers to effect the sale of unregistered shares are in violation of the Securities Act. (United States v. Wolfson)

3. **The Section 4 (1/2) Exemption.** One is not an underwriter under the 1933 Securities Act if he originally purchased his shares to hold. (Ackerberg v. Johnson)

SEC v. CHINESE CONSOLIDATED BENEVOLENT ASSOCIATION, INC.
120 F.2d 738 (2d Cir. 1941), cert. denied, 314 U.S. 618 (1941)

NATURE OF CASE: Action to restrain sale of bonds which have not been registered with the SEC.

FACT SUMMARY: A committee was formed to solicit funds from the Chinese community to purchase bonds from the Chinese government.

CONCISE RULE OF LAW: Foreign bonds must be registered. A party is an underwriter even if he is not authorized by the issuer and even if he does not receive compensation.

FACTS: A group of Chinese Americans solicited funds from the Chinese American community on the east coast. These funds were for the purchase of bonds from the Chinese government. The group was not authorized to act for the Chinese government and received no compensation. The bonds were not registered with the SEC (P). The SEC (P) sought to enjoin the activities of this group, the Chinese Consolidated Benevolent Association, Inc. (D). The district court found that the Association (D) was not an underwriter, issuer, or dealer and was exempt from § 5 of the Securities Act of 1933. Section 5 made it illegal for an issuer, underwriter, or dealer to use any method of interstate commerce or communication to effect or participate in the sale of unregistered securities.

ISSUE: Is an association an underwriter where it solicits funds for the purchase of unregistered securities if it is not authorized to do so by the issuer and no compensation is received for its activities?

HOLDING AND DECISION: (Hand, J.) Yes. Foreign bonds must be registered with the SEC (P). This is required under the Securities Act of 1933 to protect the ultimate purchasers. The Committee (D) solicited funds to purchase these bonds for value. It is immaterial whether or not they were authorized to act for the Chinese government or whether it merely accepted the benefits of their unauthorized activities. In any event, the Committee (D) was participating in the sale of an unregistered security between the issuer and a purchaser. This brings the Committee (D) within the definition of an underwriter under § 5 of the Securities Act of 1933. This section applies to the entire transaction in the sale of the security. It cannot, as urged by the Committee (D), be broken up into its component parts. The Committee's (D) activities were a necessary part of the sale and it acted as an underwriter. The order of the district court is reversed and the Committee's (D) activities are enjoined until such time as the bonds have been registered.

DISSENT: (Swan, J.) Section 5, as limited by § 4, forbids only conduct by an issuer, underwriter, or dealer. The Association (D) is none of these.

EDITOR'S ANALYSIS: The court uses a transactional analysis to hold that the Committee (D) was engaged in unauthorized activities. Under this analysis, any group or individual who uses interstate commerce to solicit purchase of unregistered securities is violating the Securities Act of 1933. Carrying the court's rationale to its logical conclusion, if a man calls a friend and solicits funds for unregistered stock he technically violates the Act.

NOTES:

UNITED STATES v. WOLFSON
405 F.2d 779 (2d Cir. 1968), cert. denied, 394 U.S. 946 (1969)

NATURE OF CASE: Appeal of conviction for violation of federal securities laws.

FACT SUMMARY: Wolfson (D) and his associates, controlling shareholders in a corporation, utilized brokers to effect the sale of unregistered shares.

CONCISE RULE OF LAW: Controlling shareholders who utilize brokers to effect the sale of unregistered shares are in violation of the Securities Act.

FACTS: Wolfson (D) and several associates owned a de facto controlling block of shares of Continental Enterprises, Inc. Over a period of time, Wolfson (D) and his associates, through several brokers, sold large blocks of unregistered Continental stock. The Justice Department instituted a criminal action against Wolfson (D) and his associates for violating registration provisions of the Securities Act. They were convicted and appealed.

ISSUE: Are controlling shareholders who utilize brokers to effect the sale of unregistered shares in violation of the Securities Act?

HOLDING AND DECISION: (Woodbury, J.) Yes. Controlling shareholders who utilize brokers to effect the sale of unregistered shares are in violation of the Securities Act. Section 5(a) of the Act makes it unlawful for any person to effect the sale of an unregistered security in a transaction involving an issuer, underwriter, or dealer. Wolfson (D) argued that the brokers were in fact not issuers, underwriters, or dealers. However, "underwriter" is statutorily defined as anyone who purchases from an issuer with a view to distribution. "Issuer" is defined at § 2(11) to include individuals controlling an issuer. Here, since Wolfson (D) controlled Continental, the brokers who bought from him were underwriters, and the transaction fell within the ambit of the Act. Affirmed.

EDITOR'S ANALYSIS: The opinion herein did not discuss the liability of the brokers themselves. As underwriters, they could be criminally liable. The Securities Act does provide a broker's exemption to liability. The exception is a narrow one, and whether the brokers could have taken advantage of this exception is not clear from the facts as stated in the opinion.

NOTES:

ACKERBERG v. JOHNSON
892 F.2d 1328 (8th Cir. 1989).

NATURE OF CASE: Appeal from judgment granting rescission of a stock purchase.

FACT SUMMARY: Johnson (D), who sold shares of stock to Ackerberg (P), had originally purchased the shares to hold, rather than distribute.

CONCISE RULE OF LAW: One is not an underwriter under the 1933 Securities Act if he originally purchased his shares to hold.

FACTS: In March of 1984, Ackerberg (P) purchased shares of stock in a company called Vermitag from Johnson (D), who had purchased his shares in an initial offering in 1979 or 1980. The stock had not been registered under the 1933 Securities Act. Dissatisfied with his investment, Ackerberg (P) later sued for rescission. Finding Johnson (D) to have been an underwriter under the Act, and therefore not entitled to an exemption under § 4(1), the district court entered summary judgment in favor of Ackerberg (P). Johnson (D) appealed.

ISSUE: Is one an underwriter under the 1933 Securities Act if he originally purchased his shares to hold?

HOLDING AND DECISION: (Beam, J.) No. One is not an underwriter under the 1933 Securities Act if he originally purchased his shares to hold. A person is an underwriter under the Act if he purchases shares with an intent to resell the shares to the public in a distribution-type manner. To determine intent, courts look to whether the security holder has held the securities long enough to negate any inference that he intended to distribute them. A three-year holding period is conclusive that securities have "come to rest," i.e., were acquired without a view to distribution. Here, Johnson (D) purchased his securities in 1979 or 1980 and did not sell them to Ackerberg (P) until 1984, a holding period long enough to establish that the securities had "come to rest." Therefore, the resell does not constitute a sale made in connection with a distribution. Absent a distribution, Johnson (D) cannot be an underwriter and is therefore exempt from registration requirements. Reversed.

EDITOR'S ANALYSIS: The length of time that shares are held is an obvious factor in analyzing whether one acted as an underwriter. The shorter the time that they are held, the more likely it is that the buyer purchased as an underwriter. As a general practice, if shares are held more than two years, it is unlikely that the purchaser will be found to have been an underwriter.

NOTES:

CHAPTER 7
RECAPITALIZATIONS, REORGANIZATIONS, AND ACQUISITIONS

QUICK REFERENCE RULES OF LAW

1. **Spinoffs and the '33 Act.** A corporation's practice of purchasing and merging private companies may violate registration provisions of the Securities Act. (SEC v. Datronics Engineers, Inc.)

SEC v. DATRONICS ENGINEERS, INC.
490 F.2d 250 (4th Cir. 1973), cert. denied, 416 U.S. 937 (1974)

NATURE OF CASE: Appeal of denial of preliminary injunction against securities laws registration violations.

FACT SUMMARY: The SEC (P) contended that Datronics Engineers, Inc.'s (D) practice of purchasing and merging private companies violated registration provisions of the Securities Act.

CONCISE RULE OF LAW: A corporation's practice of purchasing and merging private companies may violate registration provisions of the Securities Act.

FACTS: Datronics Engineers, Inc. (D) was a publicly traded corporation. On nine different occasions. Datronics (D) effected a transaction wherein a private company was merged into a subsidiary of Datronics (D), with the former owners of the private company receiving a majority interest in the subsidiary. The remainder of the stock would be distributed among shareholders in Datronics (D). The SEC (P) brought an action against Datronics (D), alleging violations of registration provisions of the Securities Act. The district court denied the SEC's (P) application for a preliminary injunction, and the SEC (P) appealed.

ISSUE: May a corporation's practice of purchasing and merging private companies violate registration provisions of the Securities Act?

HOLDING AND DECISION: (Bryan, J.) Yes. A corporation's practice of purchasing and merging private companies may violate registration provisions of the Securities Act. Section 5 of the Act prohibits use of the mails for distribution of unregistered securities "for the purpose of sale or for delivery after sale" by an issuer. Datronics (D) contended that the merger transactions were not sales, but in substance they were. The term "sale" is defined in § 2(3) of the Act to include any disposition of a security for sale. In the merger transactions, a minority of shares was disseminated among Datronics' (D) shareholders. As these shares were marketable, they had value. Consequently, the mergers involved use of the mails for unregistered sales. This constituted a violation of § 5. Due to the fact that these mergers have occurred nine times so far, the likelihood of future harm is sufficient to justify an injunction. Reversed.

CONCURRENCE: (Widener, J.) The major compelling reason for finding a § 5 violation here was that no business purpose other than creating a market for the merged corporations' stocks appeared to underlie the transaction.

EDITOR'S ANALYSIS: In this case, the form of the transaction was a stock dividend: shareholders of Datronics (D) would receive additional shares of already issued stock. In substance, this was what came to be known as a "back-door" offering, designed to evade registration requirements. This case illustrates that, in securities laws enforcement actions, substance may prevail over form.

NOTES:

CHAPTER 8
EXEMPT SECURITIES

QUICK REFERENCE RULES OF LAW

1. **Securities of Nonprofit Issuers.** An institution does not qualify for the charitable purpose exemption from registration if its organizers or owners are conducting it for their private profit or advantage. (SEC v. Children's Hospital)

2. **Variable Annuities.** Variable annuities are subject to federal securities law since they do not qualify as insurance because they do not involve risk-taking by the issuer. (SEC v. Variable Annuity Life Insurance Co.)

3. **Rule 151.** Fixed annuities with variable excess interest rates at the discretion of the issuer are not exempt from federal securities laws. (Otto v. Variable Annuity Life Insurance Co.)

SEC v. CHILDREN'S HOSPITAL
214 F. Supp. 883 (D. Ariz. 1963).

NATURE OF CASE: Action seeking to enjoin bond offering.

FACT SUMMARY: The SEC (P) contended that a bond offering of a hospital was not exempt from registration because the hospital's organizers realized a profit from its construction and operation.

CONCISE RULE OF LAW: An institution does not qualify for the charitable purpose exemption from registration if its organizers or owners are conducting it for their private profit or advantage.

FACTS: Jennings and Ross promoted the construction of Children's Hospital (D). To finance the construction, Children's Hospital (D) announced a bond offering in excess of one million dollars. Children's (D) was constructed by a contractor in which Jennings and Ross had a substantial interest. As directors, Jennings and Ross received salaries of $1,000 per month. They also planned to receive $50,000 from the bond proceeds. The SEC (P) filed an action seeking to enjoin the offering, contending that the offering was not exempt from registration under § 3(a)(4) of the Securities Act, as Children's (D) was not a charitable organization. Children's (D), in reply, argued that it admitted many patients free of charge.

ISSUE: Does an institution qualify for the charitable purpose exemption from registration if its organizers or owners are conducting it for their private profit or advantage?

HOLDING AND DECISION: (Davis, J.) No. An institution does not qualify for the charitable purpose exemption from registration if its organizers or owners are conducting it for their private profit or advantage. The main issue in the applicability of the exemption is not whether the issuer engages in charitable activities but rather whether it operates on a nonprofit basis. If individuals realize a substantial income from the institution, the charitable purpose exemption found in § 3(a)(4) of the Act is inapplicable. Here, Jennings and Ross realized $50,000 from the promotion of Children's (D) and $12,000 per year in salary. Therefore, Children's (D) is not a nonprofit operation, and the exemption is not available. Injunction granted.

EDITOR'S ANALYSIS: The decision in the present case was easy, as the facts were one-sided. However, cases of this nature can be quite complex. Clever minds can devise any number of compensation schemes not so obvious as that at issue here. Ascertaining whether an operation is truly nonprofit can thus be difficult.

NOTES:

SEC v. VARIABLE ANNUITY LIFE INSURANCE CO. OF AMERICA
359 U.S. 65 (1959).

NATURE OF CASE: Appeal from the dismissal of an action to enjoin the offering of unregistered annuities.

FACT SUMMARY: Variable Annuity Life Insurance Co. (VALIC) (D) contended that the variable annuities it offered to the public were insurance contracts that were exempt from federal securities laws.

CONCISE RULE OF LAW: Variable annuities are subject to federal securities law since they do not qualify as insurance because they do not involve risk-taking by the issuer.

FACTS: VALIC (D) offered a variable annuity program to the public. Under a variable annuity, the holder must make periodic payments which continue until the annuitant's death or the end of a fixed term. The payments vary according to the age and sex of the annuitant. The annuitant is paid from both principal and income. The income is provided from a return from investments in common stock which is supposed to compensate for inflation. VALIC (D) assumes the risk of mortality and is obligated to make annuity payments on the basis of the mortality prediction reflected in the contract but does not guarantee a fixed income. The SEC (P) filed suit to enjoin VALIC (D) from offering the variable annuities without registering them under the Securities Act of 1933. VALIC (D) responded that the variable annuities were exempt from federal securities regulations because they were insurance contracts already covered by the McCarran-Ferguson Act. The district court ruled for VALIC (D), and the SEC (P) appealed.

ISSUE: Are variable annuities subject to federal securities law?

HOLDING AND DECISION: (Douglas, J.) Yes. Variable annuities are subject to federal securities law since they do not qualify as insurance because they do not involve risk-taking by the issuer. Under the broad definition of "security" contained in the Securities Act of 1933, an annuity qualifies as a security. However, instruments that qualify as insurance contracts under the McCarran-Ferguson Act are exempt from the provisions of the Securities Act. Although the concept of insurance and annuities was developed under state law, the meaning of these terms is a federal question under the two Acts. The concept of insurance involves some investment risk-taking on the part of the issuing company. In common understanding, this means a guarantee that some of the benefits will be payable in fixed amounts. There is no true underwriting of the risk where benefits are not guaranteed in fixed amounts to some extent. VALIC's (D) variable annuities pay the holders a pro rata share of what the portfolio of equity interests reflect and, therefore, do not guarantee any fixed amount of benefits. Thus, the variable annuity offered by VALIC (D) is not an insurance contract within the meaning of the Securities Act and McCarran-Ferguson. Hence, it is not exempt from registration under the Securities Act. Reversed.

CONCURRENCE: (Brennan, J.) The policy behind the Securities Act was to emphasize disclosure in investments, a policy not found under state insurance regulations. Since variable annuities resemble open-ended investment securities, the disclosure policy of the Securities Act is required to protect investors.

DISSENT: (Harlan, J.) State regulation of insurance should be allowed to develop to encompass instruments such as the variable annuity rather than placing them within federal control.

EDITOR'S ANALYSIS: Justice Brennan's concurrence differed from the majority holding by asserting that the risk of the investor was more relevant than the lack of risk by the issuing company. Some commentators have agreed with Brennan that the degree of risk assumed by the policyholder is a more relevant factor than the presence of a fixed return. See Clark, The Regulation of Financial Holding Companies, 92 Harv. L. Rev. 787 (1979).

NOTES:

OTTO v. VARIABLE ANNUITY LIFE INSURANCE CO.
814 F.2d 1127 (7th Cir. 1986).

NATURE OF CASE: Appeal from the dismissal of a class action for violations of the Securities Exchange Act of 1934.

FACT SUMMARY: Variable Annuity Life Insurance Co. (VALIC) (D) sold a fixed annuity to Otto (P) and other class members that guaranteed 4% interest and excess interest at a rate fixed by VALIC (D).

CONCISE RULE OF LAW: Fixed annuities with variable excess interest rates at the discretion of the issuer are not exempt from federal securities laws.

FACTS: VALIC (D) offered a fixed annuity to employees of certain tax-exempt organizations. Under this annuity, VALIC (D) guaranteed the principal and a 4% interest rate for the first ten years and 3˚% thereafter. The participants were paid an excess interest rate that was set at the discretion of VALIC (D) to be a banding method. Under this method, the current rate of excess interest was only paid on deposits made during the current period. Prior payments earned the rates of excess interest declared during the period in which those contributions were made, but VALIC (D) retained the right to adjust the rate paid on past contributions. Otto (P) bought a fixed annuity from VALIC (D) and subsequently filed a class action on behalf of other purchasers, alleging that VALIC (D) did not disclose the banding method of determining the excess interest rate. VALIC (D) responded that the fixed annuity was not subject to the disclosure requirements of the Securities Exchange Act of 1934 because it was an exempt insurance contract.

ISSUE: Are fixed annuities with variable excess interest rates exempt from federal securities laws?

HOLDING AND DECISION: (Cudahy, J.) No. Fixed annuities with variable excess interest rates at the discretion of the issuer are not exempt from federal securities laws. Section 3(a)(8) of the Securities Exchange Act of 1934 provides that annuities are exempt from the provisions of the Act. Rule 151 establishes a safe harbor for certain types of annuity contracts. Under Rule 151, annuities issued by a bank or insurance company regulated at the state or federal level which are not marketed primarily as investments and which give the investment risk to the issuer are exempt from the Act. An issuer is deemed to assume the investment risk when there is a guarantee of a minimal interest rate and the specified rate is not changed more than once a year. Although Rule 151 did not become effective until after the sale of the fixed annuity to Otto (P), its reasoning may be used to interpret the scope of the exemption of § 3(a)(8). VALIC (D) is subject to the insurance laws of Texas and marketed the fixed annuity on the basis of its stability and security. However, since VALIC (D) claims to retain the unfettered discretion to alter the excess interest rate on past and future payments, it has not assumed the investment risk. Otto (P) retains an investment risk under VALIC's (D) fixed annuity because VALIC (D) can change the excess interest rate at any time. Therefore, the fixed annuity would not qualify under the safe harbor provision of Rule 151 and is not exempt under § 3(a)(8). Reversed.

EDITOR'S ANALYSIS: The court had first decided this case in favor of VALIC (D), but, on rehearing, VALIC (D) informed the court for the first time that it had the right to adjust the established excess interest rate at its discretion. The Supreme Court denied certiorari after first inviting the Solicitor General to file a brief expressing the position of the SEC. His brief argued that the holding was wrong in implying that a contract not within the safe harbor of Rule 151 was automatically not exempt under § 3(a)(8).

NOTES:

CHAPTER 9
LIABILITY UNDER THE SECURITIES ACT

QUICK REFERENCE RULES OF LAW

1. **The Defendants and Their Defenses.** Directors and officers must pursue a reasonably diligent investigation in order to avoid liability for false registration statements under § 11. (Escott v. BarChris Construction Co.)

2. **Damages.** Liability under § 11 for material misrepresentations in registration statements may be avoided or reduced by proving that the depreciation in the value of the stock resulted from other factors. (Akerman v. Oryx Communications, Inc.)

3. **Section 12(a)(1).** Liability under § 12(1) of the Securities Acts extends only to persons who successfully solicit the purchase of securities for their own personal gain or that of the securities owner. (Pinter v. Dahl)

4. **By Means of a "Prospectus or Oral Communication."** For the purposes of determining a right of rescission under § 12(2), the term "prospectus," as used in the Securities Act of 1933, refers to documents related to public offerings, not to private secondary sales. (Gustafson v. Alloyd Co.)

5. **Liability.** Underwriters of commercial paper may be liable under § 12(2) of the Securities Act if they breach the duty to reasonably investigate the issuer. (Sanders v. John Nuveen & Co.)

6. **Section 17(a).** Proof of scienter is required under § 17(a)(1) of the Securities Act but not under §§ 17(a)(2) and 17(a)(3). (Aaron v. SEC)

7. **Section 17(a).** Section 17(a) of the Securities Act does not provide a private remedy. (In re Washington Public Power Supply System Securities Litigation)

ESCOTT v. BARCHRIS CONSTRUCTION CO.
283 F. Supp. 643 (S.D.N.Y. 1968).

NATURE OF CASE: Action for violation of § 11 of the Securities Act of 1933.

FACT SUMMARY: The purchasers (P) of debentures issued by BarChris (D) alleged that the directors and officers of BarChris (D) were responsible for false statements and material omissions in the registration statement.

CONCISE RULE OF LAW: Directors and officers must pursue a reasonably diligent investigation in order to avoid liability for false registration statements under § 11.

FACTS: BarChris (D) built bowling centers for customers who made a comparatively small down payment and paid the balance of the contract price in notes payable over a period of years. In order to finance this operation, BarChris (D) was in constant need of new cash. In 1961, BarChris (D) filed a registration statement for convertible subordinated fifteen-year debentures, which became effective on May 16. At that time, BarChris (D) was experiencing difficulties in collecting amounts due on past construction because the bowling industry was overbuilt. BarChris (D) continued to construct new bowling alleys despite the fact that operators began to fail and default. Finally, in 1962, BarChris (D) filed for bankruptcy and defaulted on the payments of interest due on the debentures. The purchasers (P) of the debentures filed suit against the directors and officers of BarChris (D), including Birnbaum (D), a young lawyer hired as house counsel, Auslander (D), an outside director, Grant (D), a director who wrote the registration statement, and Peat, Marwick (D) the accountants. The purchasers (P) alleged that the registration statement misrepresented income figures, understated their contingent liability on notes, and incorrectly listed orders that were not then in existence.

ISSUE: Are directors and officers required to pursue a reasonably diligent investigation in order to avoid liability for false registration statements under § 11?

HOLDING AND DECISION: (McLean, J.) Yes. Directors and officers must pursue a reasonably diligent investigation in order to avoid liability for false registration statements under § 11. Section 11 of the Securities Act subjects the issuer to strict liability for damages caused by material misrepresentations or omissions in a registration statement. Other persons associated with the distribution, such as the signers of the statement, the directors of the issuer, accountants who prepared materials serving as the basis for the statement, and the underwriters, are also subject to liability but may assert a due diligence defense. Experts, such as accountants and lawyers, are responsible for conducting a reasonable investigation with respect to the expertise portion of the registration statement. Directors and underwriters may rely on the expert's opinion for the expertise portion but must reasonably investigate other facts asserted in the statement. BarChris's (D) accountants, Peat, Marwick (D), did not conduct a complete audit of BarChris (D) and failed to note danger signals in the materials that were examined before providing financial figures which formed the basis of the 1961 registration statement. Therefore, Peat, Marwick (D) failed to undertake a reasonable investigation as required to assert the due diligence defense. The directors such as Birnbaum (D), Auslander (D), and Grant (D) were entitled to rely on the information audited by Peat, Marwick (D) for the expertise portion of the statement. However, they did not take any steps to investigate the truth of other statements in the registration document. Thus, these directors (D) also do not qualify for the due diligence defense. Therefore, since the misrepresentations in the registration statement for the debentures were material, BarChris (D) and the other persons associated with the registration are jointly and severally liable under § 11 to the purchasers (P).

EDITOR'S ANALYSIS: The court also held the underwriters of the BarChris (D) debentures liable even though they were misled by the directors and officers of BarChris (D). The court ruled that a reasonable investigation by underwriters should entail more than accurate reporting of the data presented to them by the company. The decision also imposed a sliding scale of diligence on directors depending on their status as management insiders or non-management outsiders.

NOTES:

AKERMAN v. ORYX COMMUNICATIONS INC.
810 F.2d 336 (2nd Cir. 1987).

NATURE OF CASE: Appeal from summary judgment in an action for damages for violation of the Securities Act.

FACT SUMMARY: Akerman (P), a purchaser of Oryx (D) stock, claimed that an inadvertent error on a registration statement caused the stock price to drop.

CONCISE RULE OF LAW: Liability under § 11 for material misrepresentations in registration statements may be avoided or reduced by proving that the depreciation in the value of the stock resulted from other factors.

FACTS: In June 1981, Oryx (D), a business that manufactured and marketed video cassettes and discs, filed a registration statement for an initial public offering of 700,000 shares of stock. The stock sold at $4.75. The prospectus within the registration statement contained an error whereby Oryx (D) posted a substantial transaction by a subsidiary in March rather than April. Thus, the prospectus overstated earnings for the period included in the financial statement. Oryx (D) reported the misstatement to the SEC on October 13, 1981, when the stock was selling at $4.00. On November 9, 1981, the day before Oryx (D) disclosed the mistake to the public, the stock was down to $3.25. Akerman (P) commenced a suit on November 25, while the stock was trading at $3.50, to recover the difference in value between the original purchase price and the value at the time the suit was initiated under § 11 of the Securities Act. Oryx (D) responded that depreciation in value resulted from factors other than the misstatement in the registration statement. The district court granted summary judgment to Oryx (D), and Akerman (P) appealed.

ISSUE: May liability under § 11 for material misrepresentations in registration statements be avoided or reduced by proving that the depreciation in the value of the stock resulted from other factors?

HOLDING AND DECISION: (Meskill, J.) Yes. Liability under § 11 for material misrepresentations in registration statements may be avoided or reduced by proving that the depreciation in the value of the stock resulted from other factors. Section 11(a) of the Securities Act imposes civil liability for damages caused to purchasers of the securities on the issuer and signatories of a registration statement that contains material misrepresentations or omissions. However, under § 11(e), defendants may reduce their liability by proving that the depreciation in the value of the stock was not caused by the material misstatements. Under § 11(e), the defendants carry a heavy burden of proving that other factors caused the depreciation in value because Congress desired to allocate the risk of uncertainty to the issuers rather than the purchasers. Oryx (D) presented evidence that the misstatement made in the registration statement was barely material because the prospectus contained a pessimistic forecast of the performance of its subsidiary. Thus, the accounting error was unlikely to have altered perceptions about performance. Furthermore, the price of Oryx's (D) stock actually rose after the error was disclosed to the public. Akerman's (P) evidence that other stocks did not do as poorly as Oryx (D) in the same period is not entitled to weight because it does not reflect any of the countless variables that might affect stock performance. Therefore, Oryx (D) met the burden of proving that factors other than registration statement error caused the depreciation in the stock. Affirmed.

EDITOR'S ANALYSIS: Akerman (P) argued that the date of the disclosure of the error to the SEC should have controlled for purposes of damages because Oryx's (D) insiders with access to the information could have sold their stock before public disclosure. The court noted that there was no evidence of insider trading and rejected this argument. In general, § 11 creates a presumption in favor of rescission damages based on the difference in value between the offering price and the market value at the time of the suit.

NOTES:

PINTER v. DAHL
486 U.S. 622 (1988).

NATURE OF CASE: Appeal from a judgment denying damages in action for violations of § 12 of the Securities Act.

FACT SUMMARY: Pinter (D), the seller of interests in an oil drilling venture, asserted a counterclaim for contribution against Dahl (P) for soliciting other investors to buy into the venture.

CONCISE RULE OF LAW: Liability under § 12(1) of the Securities Acts extends only to persons who successfully solicit the purchase of securities for their own personal gain or that of the securities owner.

FACTS: Pinter (D), an oil and gas producer, met with Dahl (P), a real estate broker, about investing in oil and gas leases. Dahl (P) invested $310,000 in Pinter's (D) Black Gold Oil Company to acquire properties. Dahl (P) then solicited other purchasers (P) to invest money in the venture but received no commission in connection with these investments. Pinter (D) sold the participating interests without registering them under the Securities Act. The venture failed, and Dahl (P) and the other purchasers (P) filed suit against Pinter (D), seeking rescission under § 12 of the Securities Act for selling unregistered securities. Pinter (D) counterclaimed against Dahl (P), alleging that Dahl (P) had induced Pinter (D) to sell the securities through misrepresentations. The trial court denied Pinter's (D) contribution on the basis that Dahl (P) was not a seller under § 12. Pinter (D) appealed.

ISSUE: Does liability under § 12(1) extend to a person who urges the purchase of security but whose motivation is solely to benefit the buyer?

HOLDING AND DECISION: (Blackmun, J.) No. Liability under § 12(1) of the Securities Acts extends only to persons who successfully solicit the purchase of securities for their own personal gain or that of the securities owner. Section 12(1) provides that any person who offers or sells a security in violation of the registration requirement shall be liable to the purchaser. This language contemplates a buyer-seller relationship similar to traditional contractual privity. Persons who do not pass title or the interest in a security may be included within the class of defendants only in certain circumstances. Since the language of § 12 includes persons who make offers to sell, an individual engaged in solicitation is within the scope of the Act. This interpretation is consistent with the purpose of the Act to promote full and fair disclosure of information to the public in the sales of securities. However, persons who offer gratuitous advice or urge another person to make a particular investment are not sellers or offerers within the meaning of § 12. Liability only extends to solicitors who are motivated by financial gain. Although Dahl (P) did not receive a commission for soliciting the sales of the securities sold by Pinter (D), the evidence does not clearly indicate whether Dahl (P) sought to receive financial benefit from the investments for himself or for Pinter (D). Therefore, the judgment is vacated, and the case is remanded to determine Dahl's (P) motivation for the solicitations.

EDITOR'S ANALYSIS: Section 12 imposes strict liability on the sellers of unregistered securities. Furthermore, the plaintiff is not required to prove injury in order to gain rescission. An illegal offer also creates a right to rescission even if the subsequent sale conforms with the registration requirements.

NOTES:

GUSTAFSON v. ALLOYD CO.
115 S.Ct. 1061 (1995).

NATURE OF CASE: Appeal from grant of right of rescission in private securities sale.

FACT SUMMARY: Alloyd Co. (P) sought to rescind its purchase of Alloyd, Inc. from Gustafson (D) under § 12(2) of the Securities Act of 1933 due to misstatements in the contract of sales.

CONCISE RULE OF LAW: For the purposes of determining a right of rescission under § 12(2), the term "prospectus," as used in the Securities Act of 1933, refers to documents related to public offerings, not to private secondary sales.

FACTS: Gustafson (D) and two other individuals were the sole shareholders of Alloyd, Inc., a manufacturer of plastic packaging and heat sealing equipment. In 1989, certain investors, now known as Alloyd Co. (P) contracted to buy out Gustafson (D) and the coshareholders (D). Due to uncertainties in the current financial status of Alloyd, Inc., the contract specified that if the estimates did not follow fact, the disappointed party was entitled to an adjustment when new hard figures became available. Under this clause, Alloyd Co. (P) became entitled to $815,000 a year later but instead brought suit in district court to rescind the contract under § 12(2) of the Securities Act of 1933. Although Gustafson (D) paid the adjustment, Alloyd Co. (P) persisted, claiming that the contract of sale was a "prospectus" so that any misstatements in it gave rise to § 12(2) liability. The district court, relying on a Third Circuit ruling, granted Gustafson's (D) summary judgment motion, holding that § 12(2) claims can only arise out of initial public offerings, not secondary private sales. The Seventh Circuit reversed, reading the Act's § 2(10) definition of "prospectus" to cover any communication offering securities for sale. The Supreme Court granted certiorari to resolve the conflict.

ISSUE: For the purposes of determining a right of rescission under § 12(2), does the term "prospectus" as used in the Securities Act of 1933 refer only to documents related to public offerings?

HOLDING AND DECISION: (Kennedy, J.) Yes. For the purposes of determining a right of rescission under § 12(2), the term "prospectus" as used in the Securities Act of 1933 refers only to documents related to public offerings. Three sections of the 1933 Act are relevant to a determination of the meaning of the word "prospectus": § 2(10), the definition; § 10, the information required in one; and § 12, which imposes liability for misstatements in one. The meaning should be consistent throughout. Section 10 confines the term to documents that must include the information from the registration statement. A registration statement is required, for the most part, only in public offerings. Read consistently, § 12(2) liability attaches only when there is a § 10 requirement to issue the prospectus, as in a public offering. The argument that any offer is a prospectus under § 12 would require a holding that the term is broader in § 12 than in § 10. This argument arises from the definition of the term in § 2(10), which provides that "[t]he term 'prospectus' means any prospectus, notice, circular, advertisement, letter, or communication, written or by radio or television, which offers any security for sale or confirms the sale of any security." Alloyd Co. (P) and the dissent rely on the word "communication" to give prospectus a broad definition, yet they fail to consider the public nature of the § 2(10) list. In context, the list refers to documents of wide dissemination, but leaves out face-to-face and phone conversations. Congress provided the right to rescind in § 12(2) for documents prepared under investigation with established procedures in the context of a public offering. It is not plausible to believe that Congress intended every casual communication in the secondary market to grant a right of rescission absent evidence of fraud or reliance. Legislative history supports this interpretation. Reversed.

DISSENT: (Thomas, J.) The congressionally provided broad definition of "prospectus" in § 2(10) should be used to find the term's meaning, rather than using the 1933 Act to fit the definition as the majority does. The majority analysis is motivated by the assumption that Congress would never have imposed § 12(2) liability on the secondary market, and that public policy would like to avoid unwanted increases in litigation. Yet the majority forgets we are only enforcing Congress' decision about standards of conduct for sellers and that it is up to the other branches of government to limit the 1933 Act.

DISSENT: (Ginsburg, J.) The Securities Act was modeled on the British Companies Act of 1929. In adopting a definition of "prospectus" from that Act, the language limiting it to communications "offering [securities] to the public" is conspicuously omitted. This omission suggests that the drafters of the 1933 Act intended the term "prospectus" to reach beyond public offerings.

EDITOR'S ANALYSIS: If § 12(2) encompassed secondary sales yet maintained its negligence standard, it would eclipse § 10b(5) and overwhelm the legal system with lawsuits. The case above makes clear that nobody except the plaintiffs wanted this, but the argument is whether the majority rewrote the definition of "prospectus" or merely interpreted it. This case is new and the fallout incomplete as yet, but it is safe to say that "prospectus" will continue to have the same meaning it has had for the last sixty years by way of this case or an act of Congress.

NOTES:

SANDERS v. JOHN NUVEEN & CO.
619 F.2d 1222 (7th Cir. 1980).

NATURE OF CASE: Class action for damages under § 12 of the Securities Act.

FACT SUMMARY: The purchasers (P) of unsecured short-term promissory notes issued by Winter & Hirsch (WH) contended that John Nuveen & Co. (D), the underwriter, was liable under § 12 after WH's default.

CONCISE RULE OF LAW: Underwriters of commercial paper may be liable under § 12(2) of the Securities Act if they breach the duty to reasonably investigate the issuer.

FACTS: Winter & Hirsch (WH), a consumer finance company, issued unsecured short-term promissory notes in 1969. John Nuveen & Co. (D) was the exclusive underwriter of the WH notes and sold the commercial paper through its offices across the country. Nuveen (D) prepared and circulated to prospective customers a commercial paper report on the WH notes. Some of the purchasers (P) who bought the notes from Nuveen (D) read those reports, while others were given oral statements about the quality of the WH notes. Other purchasers (P) did not receive any information. WH began issuing false financial statements in the ten years prior to the issuance of the notes with the help of its accountants. By 1970, WH's financial statements had significantly overstated its accounts receivable, and WH was forced to default on the notes in 1970. The purchasers (P) of the notes sold by Nuveen (D) in the period leading up to the default filed suit against Nuveen (D) for failing to investigate WH's financial condition. Nuveen (D) responded that the purchasers (P) who had not received the commercial paper reports were barred from recovery for lack of reliance and also that Nuveen (D) could not have known of WH's fraud.

ISSUE: Are underwriters required to make reasonable inquiries to discover the possibility of fraud by the issuer of commercial paper under § 12(2) of the Securities Act?

HOLDING AND DECISION: (Tone, J.) Yes. Underwriters of commercial paper may be liable under § 12(2) of the Securities Act if they breach the duty to reasonably investigate the issuer. Section 12(2) of the Securities Act of 1933 imposes liability on any person who sells a security by means of a prospectus or oral communication containing material misrepresentations. This language means that there must be some causal connection between the misleading statement and the purchase of the security. However, the purchaser does not need to prove reliance on a misrepresentation in order to recover under §12(2). Thus, the causation requirement is satisfied when the misleading statements affect the market trading price regardless of whether an individual purchaser was aware of the misleading statement. Therefore, since Nuveen (D) released a commercial paper report on WH to the public, its trading price reflected the misrepresentations, and the purchasers (P) were affected regardless of whether they received or read the report. Furthermore, under §12(2), underwriters have a duty to make reasonable inquiries that would lead to the discovery of the issuer's fraud. This requires an underwriter, who has access to more information than brokers, to investigate further than the published data provided by the issuer. Nuveen (D) did not undertake a reasonable inquiry into WH beyond the reports provided by WH. Therefore, it did not discharge its duty under § 12(2). Affirmed.

EDITOR'S ANALYSIS: Justice Powell dissented from a denial of certiorari by the Supreme Court in this case. He argued that underwriters should be entitled to rely on the accuracy of certified financial statements because it was not negligent to do so. The court in Franklin Savings Bank v. Levy, 551 F.2d 521 (2nd Cir. 1977), also approved of a negligence standard for underwriters.

NOTES:

AARON v. SEC
446 U.S. 680 (1979).

NATURE OF CASE: Appeal from a judgment for violating federal securities law.

FACT SUMMARY: The SEC (P) contended that Aaron (D), a supervisor in an investment firm, sold stock based upon unfounded recommendations and failed to stop after the issuer informed him of the improprieties.

CONCISE RULE OF LAW: Proof of scienter is required under § 17(a)(1) of the Securities Act but not under §§ 17(a)(2) and 17(a)(3).

FACTS: The investment firm of E.L. Aaron & Co. (D) recommended and sold stock based upon unfounded claims. The issuer of the stock informed Aaron (D) and other salespeople that they were selling the securities with inaccurate statements, but Aaron (D) continued the fraud. The SEC (P) filed an enforcement action against Aaron (D) under Rule 10b-5 and § 17(a) of the Securities Act. The district court found that Aaron (D) had knowingly aided and abetted the fraud. The court of appeals decided it did not need to reach the intent question because § 17(a) only required a showing of negligence in enforcement actions. Aaron (D) appealed this holding.

ISSUE: Is proof of scienter required under § 17(a) of the Securities Act?

HOLDING AND DECISION: (Stewart, J.) Yes. Proof of scienter is required under § 17(a)(1) of the Securities Act but not under §§ 17(a)(2) and 17(a)(3). Congress intended securities legislation to be construed flexibly in order to effectuate its remedial purposes. However, where the language of a provision is sufficiently clear in its context, it is unnecessary to examine policy considerations in order to determine the meaning of the provision. The language of § 17(a) strongly suggests that Congress intended a scienter requirement under § 17(a)(1) because it states that it is unlawful to "employ any device, scheme, or artifice to defraud." These terms plainly connote knowing or intentional practices. By contrast, the language of § 17(a)(2) prohibits the obtaining of money by any untrue statements. Nothing in this language evinces an intent requirement. Finally, the language of § 17(a)(3), prohibiting any person from engaging in a practice that "operates or would operate as a fraud," plainly focuses on the effect of conduct rather than on the culpability of the person responsible. Thus, there is no scienter requirement in this subparagraph. This result is not inconsistent with § 17(a) because each subparagraph was meant to proscribe distinct categories of misconduct. The decision by the court of appeals is reversed, and the case is remanded for a determination in light of this decision.

EDITOR'S ANALYSIS: Prior to this decision, it was generally assumed that § 17(a) was unnecessary because Rule 10b-5 was drawn directly from § 17(a) but also extended to fraudulent purchases. However, the scope of Rule 10b-5 began to be restricted by the courts, and this decision gave effect to statutory differences. Now, the SEC (P) often uses § 17(a) when state of mind is at issue.

NOTES:

IN RE WASHINGTON PUBLIC POWER SUPPLY SYSTEM SECURITIES LITIGATION
823 F.2d 1349 (9th Cir. 1987).

NATURE OF CASE: Appeal from the dismissal of a private action under § 17(a) of the Securities Act for fraud.

FACT SUMMARY: The purchasers (P) of bonds issued by Washington Public Power Supply System (WPPSS) (D) sought to bring a class action under § 17(a) of the Securities Act.

CONCISE RULE OF LAW: Section 17(a) of the Securities Act does not provide a private remedy.

FACTS: WPPSS (D) sold bonds with a face value of $2.25 billion to finance two nuclear power plants from 1977 to 1981. In 1982, WPPSS (D) defaulted on the bond payments. In 1983, the purchasers (P) of the bonds instituted a class action against WPPSS (D), alleging that the bonds were sold on false pretenses. The purchasers (P) made claims under § 17(a) of the Securities Act. The district court dismissed these claims, but the court of appeals reversed. The entire court of appeals granted a rehearing on the issue.

ISSUE: Does § 17(a) of the Securities Act provide for a private remedy?

HOLDING AND DECISION: (Hall, J.) No. Section 17(a) of the Securities Act does not provide a private remedy. The Supreme Court in Cort v. Ash, 422 U.S. 66 (1975), set out the factors that must be considered in determining whether a statute implies a private remedy where it is not expressly granted. The critical considerations are the intent of Congress and whether the remedy would be consistent with the legislative scheme. The language of § 17(a) of the Securities Act represents a general censure of fraudulent practices and provides the SEC with specific procedures to enforce the provisions. The language of § 17(a) does not reveal any intent to create a private remedy. Moreover, the inclusion in §§ 11 and 12 of the Securities Act of a private remedy demonstrates that Congress expressly provided for a remedy where it desired one. Furthermore, barring private actions under §17(a) would not result in fraudulent practices going undetected and unremedied. Plaintiffs have the option of pursuing the same claims under Section 10(b) of the Securities Exchange Act of 1934. Therefore, there is no basis for inferring a private right of action from the language of §17(a) or the legislative scheme in which it is contained. Thus, the dismissal of the purchasers' (P) claims against WPPSS (D) was proper. Reversed.

DISSENT: (Tang, J.) The private right of action under § 17(a) has been allowed for thirty-eight years and should not be overturned because courts sense a Supreme Court trend toward restricting private remedies.

EDITOR'S ANALYSIS: This decision is in accord with the majority view on private remedies under § 17(a). Prior to the decision in Aaron v. Securities and Exchange Commission, 446 U.S. 680 (1979), courts summarily allowed the actions as redundant to Rule 10b-5 actions. However, once the decision in Aaron separated the scope of § 17(a) from Rule 10b-5, courts were forced to reconsider their decision to allow private § 17(a) actions.

NOTES:

CHAPTER 10
THE SECURITIES EXCHANGE ACT OF 1934: MARKETS AND INFORMATION

QUICK REFERENCE RULES OF LAW

1. **The Relationship of Section 9(a) to Rule 10b-5.** A person cannot be convicted of manipulating stock prices if a subjective intent to manipulate such prices cannot be shown. (United States v. Mulheren)

2. **Compliance.** The SEC may impose liability under the Foreign Corrupt Practices Act when internal accounting records and controls are inadequate, without proof of scienter. (SEC v. World-Wide Coin Investment Ltd.)

UNITED STATES v. MULHEREN
938 F.2d 364 (2d Cir. 1991).

NATURE OF CASE: Appeal of conviction for federal securities laws violations.

FACT SUMMARY: Mulheren (D) was accused of purchasing stock with the intent of manipulating its price.

CONCISE RULE OF LAW: A person cannot be convicted of manipulating stock prices if a subjective intent to manipulate such prices cannot be shown.

FACTS: Mulheren (D) was acquainted with Boesky, a high-profile Wall Street speculator. At one point Mulheren (D) had a phone conversation in which Boesky said it would be "great" if Gulf-Western stock, then trading at just over $44 per share, rose to $45. There was no evidence that Mulheren (D) knew that Boesky owned 3.4 million shares. Boesky, who testified at trial, did not so imply. Mulheren (D) not long thereafter purchased 75,000 shares for Jamie, his client. This caused Gulf-Western stock to rise to $45, whereupon Boesky sold. Subsequently, the Justice Department indicted Mulheren (D) for violating § 10(b) of the Exchange Act by purchasing with the intent to affect stock prices, which it held to be a form of securities fraud. Mulheren (D) was convicted, and he appealed.

ISSUE: Can a person be convicted of manipulating stock prices if a subjective intent to manipulate such prices cannot be shown?

HOLDING AND DECISION: (McLaughlin, J.) No. A person cannot be convicted of manipulating stock prices if a subjective intent to manipulate such prices cannot be shown. It is questionable whether trading in securities with the sole intent to manipulate prices is in fact illegal. Assuming this, it is necessary that the Government (P) prove such intent beyond a reasonable doubt. Here, the Government (P) has failed to do this. The main piece of evidence was Boesky's conversation with Mulheren (D) that it would be "great" if Gulf-Western stock rose to $45 per share and Mulheren's (D) subsequent purchase. The Government (P) introduced no evidence that Mulheren (D) was aware of Boesky's holdings or that there was any quid pro quo. To convict Mulheren (D), the Government (P) had to prove that Mulheren (D) intended to manipulate rather than invest, and such proof was not made. Reversed.

EDITOR'S ANALYSIS: The court premised its decision on the assumption that trading for the sole purpose of manipulating prices constitutes a § 10(b) violation. However, from dicta, it appears that the court was ill-disposed to read § 10(b) in this manner. The issue has not been decided by the Supreme Court as yet, so courts of appeal have no higher guidance on this issue.

NOTES:

SEC v. WORLD-WIDE COIN INVESTMENTS LTD.
567 F. Supp. 724 (N.D. Ga. 1983).

NATURE OF CASE: Action for a permanent injunction against securities fraud practices.

FACT SUMMARY: The SEC (P) alleged that World-Wide's (D) internal accounting practices violated the Foreign Corrupt Practices Act (FCPA), which incorporated accounting provisions into federal securities laws.

CONCISE RULE OF LAW: The SEC may impose liability under the Foreign Corrupt Practices Act when internal accounting records and controls are inadequate, without proof of scienter.

FACTS: World-Wide Coin (D) was engaged in wholesale and retail sale of rare coins, precious metal, and Coca-Cola collector items. Sales are transacted at its Atlanta office and at coin shows throughout the country. World-Wide's (D) common stock was registered with the SEC (P) and listed on the Boston Stock Exchange until 1981. In July 1979, when Hale (D) took over management and control, World-Wide (D) had forty employees and over $2 million in assets. Shortly thereafter, Kanes, Benator, an independent auditor, warned Hale (D) that World-Wide's (D) internal accounting system was inadequate with regard to inventory and records, but Hale (D) ignored the advice. World-Wide (D) employees were not required to write purchase orders, and rare coins were left unguarded at all times, making it impossible to have an accurate inventory count. Subsequently, World-Wide (D) experienced financial difficulties due to problems caused by the lack of internal accounting controls. In August 1981, the SEC (P) filed suit against World-Wide (D) and Hale (D), alleging violations of the Securities Exchange Act of 1934.

ISSUE: May the SEC impose liability under the FCPA when internal accounting records and controls are inadequate?

HOLDING AND DECISION: (Vining, J.) Yes. The SEC (P) may impose liability under the FCPA when internal accounting records and controls are inadequate, without proof of scienter. The FCPA incorporated accounting provisions into federal securities law and allows the SEC (P) enforcement over the internal accounting procedures of companies who have registered securities. The FCPA reflects Congress's intention that the scope of federal securities laws must be expanded beyond disclosure requirements. Section 13(b)(2)(a) of the FCPA contains the books and records provision whereby company records must reflect transactions in conformity with accepted accounting methods; misrepresentations and concealment which result in inaccurate records are made unlawful. The requirement for accuracy of records expects only that the record-keeping system will be adequate and leaves it to the company to decide how the system should be implemented. The FCPA does not contain any specific standards and recognizes that the costs of internal controls do not have to exceed the benefits that will be derived. The size of the business, its complexity, and other circumstances are proper considerations when determining whether internal accounting procedures are adequate. Also, there is no scienter requirement contained in §13(b)(2)(a) since even inadvertent errors could cause the unauthorized use of corporate assets that Congress sought to prevent through the FCPA. World-Wide (D) and Hale (D) were explicitly warned by independent auditors that their accounting system had significant weaknesses. World-Wide (D) was subsequently virtually destroyed, in part because of the lack of internal accounting controls. Therefore, World-Wide's (D) accounting procedures clearly were inadequate according to the FCPA. An independent auditing is ordered, Hale (D) must return all shares of World-Wide (D) that he holds, and World-Wide (D) must disclose all material information relating to its operations since July 1979. Judgment for the SEC (P).

EDITOR'S ANALYSIS: The powers granted to the SEC under the FCPA allows the SEC wide discretion in questioning the information process in any publicly held corporation. Faced with widespread criticism of this discretion as interfering with corporate management, the SEC has not been aggressive in pursuing cases. It has voluntarily restricted its enforcement actions to situations in which top management is involved and to unreasonable deviations that are more than occasional, inadvertent errors.

NOTES:

Notes

CHAPTER 11
FRAUD IN CONNECTION WITH THE PURCHASE OR SALE OF A SECURITY

QUICK REFERENCE RULES OF LAW

1. **The "In Connection With" Requirement.** A violation of Rule 10b-5 occurs whenever assertions are made in a manner reasonably calculated to influence the investing public. (SEC v. Texas Gulf Sulphur Co.)

2. **Scienter: Beyond Hochfelder.** Recklessness satisfies the scienter requirement of Rule 10b-5. (Backman v. Polaroid Corp.)

3. **The Publicly Held Company.** A duty to disclose arises whenever secret information renders prior public statements materially misleading, not merely when that information completely negates the public statements. (In re Time Warner Securities Litigation)

4. **The Closely Held Corporation.** Close corporations may not buy their own stock from employees without informing them of new events that substantially affect the value of the stock. (Jordan v. Duff & Phelps, Inc.)

5. **Standing to Sue.** Standing under § 10(b) of the Securities Exchange Act of 1934 and Rule 10b-5 is limited to purchasers and sellers of securities. (Cowin v. Bresler)

6. **The Analytical Framework.** In order to recover under Rule 10b-5, a plaintiff must show that reasonable reliance on a misrepresentation or omission caused the loss. (Huddleston v. Herman & MacLean)

7. **The Fraud on the Market Theory.** A rebuttable presumption of reliance is appropriate where misrepresentations have caused fraud-on-the-market under Rule 10b-5. (Basic, Inc. v. Levinson)

8. **Face-to-Face Transactions.** Under Rule 10b-5, defrauded sellers are entitled to the difference between the fair value of what was received and the fair value of what would have been received if there had been no fraudulent conduct. (Rowe v. Maremont Corp.)

SECURITIES AND EXCHANGE COMMISSION v. TEXAS GULF SULPHUR CO.

401 F.2d 833 (2d Cir. 1968) (en banc), cert denied, 394 U.S. 976 (1969).

NATURE OF CASE: Appeal of trial court dismissal of a charge of Rule 10b-5 violations.

FACT SUMMARY: A Texas Gulf Sulphur Co. (D) press release drastically downplayed a major copper ore discovery, suggesting no ore was uncovered.

CONCISE RULE OF LAW: A violation of Rule 10b-5 occurs whenever assertions are made in a manner reasonably calculated to influence the investing public.

FACTS: Texas Gulf Sulphur Co. (D) was conducting exploratory mining activity by drilling core samples. An especially good site was discovered, and TGS's (D) president, Stephens (D), ordered the find kept secret until more surrounding land could be acquired. As more cores were drilled to identify the scope of the ore field, rumors of the find began circulating. Stephens (D) ordered a press release drafted which stated that the drilling to date was inconclusive at best. No identifiable securities trades were conducted by the officers of TGS (D) during this period, and the stock price was fairly stable. The SEC (P) charged TGS (D) with a violation of Rule 10b-5. At trial, the SEC (P) claim was dismissed, and the SEC (P) appealed.

ISSUE: Does a violation of Rule 10b-5 occur whenever assertions are made in a manner reasonably calculated to influence the investing public?

HOLDING AND DECISION: (Court en banc) Yes. A violation of Rule 10b-5 occurs whenever assertions are made in a manner reasonably calculated to influence the investing public. Rule 10b-5 is designed to protect the investing public from misleading information; if the market does not react to a misleading statement, the issuance is still a violation of Rule 10b-5. In this case, the press statement, which virtually denied the projected value of the find, violated Rule 10b-5 because it attempted to influence the investing public. Remanded for further proceedings to determine whether the press release was false and misleading.

EDITOR'S ANALYSIS: At the time this case was decided, the Supreme Court had not yet ruled that only intentional misrepresentations or omissions are actionable. Under that standard, TGS (D) would have probably escaped liability since their concern was with land aquisition, not deception of the trading public. Obviously, the price for the land would have skyrocketed if it were known that one of the largest ore deposits in North America was just under the surface.

NOTES:

BACKMAN v. POLAROID CORP.
893 F.2d 1405 (1st Cir. 1990).

NATURE OF CASE: Appeal from an award of damages in an action for violation of Rule 10b-5.

FACT SUMMARY: Stockholders (P) of Polaroid (D) alleged that the market price of their stock was artificially inflated because Polaroid (D) failed to disclose material information concerning sales difficulties with Polavision.

CONCISE RULE OF LAW: Recklessness satisfies the scienter requirement of Rule 10b-5.

FACTS: In 1978, Polaroid (D) began national sales of an instant motion picture system called Polavision. Polaroid's (D) Third Quarter Report in 1978 emphasized record earnings but acknowledged substantial expenses associated with Polavision. These expenses were due to sales of Polavision well below expectations. Polaroid (D) subsequently requested that its supplier cut production without informing the public. Internal forecasts by Polaroid (D) in late 1978 calculated that earnings would be significantly less than most market analysts were predicting. Meanwhile, a foundation created by Polaroid's (D) founder sold 300,000 shares of stock five weeks before Polaroid (D) issued a press release announcing its latest earnings. The price of the stock went down nearly $10 after the unexpectedly low earnings. Stockholders (P) brought a suit under Rule 10b-5, alleging that Polaroid (D) had failed to disclose material information about Polavision, which in turn artificially raised the stock price before the February announcement. The jury awarded damages to the stockholders (P), and Polaroid (D) appealed, contending that the jury instruction allowing recklessness to constitute scienter was incorrect.

ISSUE: Does recklessness satisfy the scienter requirement of Rule 10b-5?

HOLDING AND DECISION: (Bownes, J.) Yes. Recklessness satisfies the scienter requirement of Rule 10b-5. In Ernst & Ernst v. Hochfelder, 425 U.S. 185 (1976), the Supreme Court expressly defined the scienter requirement in actions brought for securities fraud. The Court held that there must be an intent to deceive, manipulate, or defraud. The Court expressly declined to determine whether recklessness was sufficient. However, eight circuit courts of appeal have determined that recklessness is sufficient. Rule 10b-5 is grounded in common law fraud where recklessness is sufficient for liability. Acts that are so highly unreasonable and such an extreme departure from the standard of ordinary care as to present a danger of misleading a plaintiff to the extent that the danger was known or should have been known to the defendant constitute recklessness. Good faith is a defense to scienter in actions for securities fraud under Rule 10b-5. The concept of the good-faith defense is implicit in any instruction as to intentional deception but is not implicit in an instruction regarding recklessness. This is because a person can act objectively reckless while acting in subjective good faith. Therefore, although the trial court gave an adequate recklessness instruction, it was error, although not reversible, to not have instructed the jury explicitly on the good-faith defense. Affirmed.

EDITOR'S ANALYSIS: The holding by the panel in this case was reversed by the court of appeals sitting en banc on rehearing on other grounds. Most courts have held that defendants do not have to desire to mislead investors in order to satisfy the scienter requirement. They must only be aware of the true facts and recognize the capacity of a statement or omission to be misleading.

NOTES:

IN RE TIME WARNER, INC. SECURITIES LITIGATION
9 F.3d 259 (2d Cir. 1993).

NATURE OF CASE: Appeal from the dismissal of a securities fraud complaint.

FACT SUMMARY: After Time Warner (D) made public statements in connection with various methods it put forward as a means of reducing its debt, shareholders (P) filed an action for securities fraud, alleging that Time Warner (D) had made material misrepresentations and omissions in its public statements.

CONCISE RULE OF LAW: A duty to disclose arises whenever secret information renders prior public statements materially misleading, not merely when that information completely negates the public statements.

FACTS: Due to a merger in which Time (D) acquired Warner Communications, Time Warner (D), the resulting entity, found itself saddled with over $10 billion in debt. Time Warner (D) then conducted a highly publicized campaign to raise capital through international "strategic partners." Because Time Warner (D) formed only two such partnerships, it was forced to seek an alternative method of raising capital through a new stock offering that substantially diluted the rights of the existing shareholders. The SEC rejected Time Warner's (D) variable price offering but approved a second proposal. Announcement of the two proposals caused a substantial decline in the price of Time Warner (D) stock. The shareholders' (P) securities fraud complaint alleged that Time Warner (D) misled the investing public by statements and omissions made with scienter. The district court dismissed the complaint with prejudice for failure to adequately plead the allegations. The shareholders (P) appealed.

ISSUE: Does a duty to disclose arise whenever secret information renders prior public statements materially misleading, not merely when that information completely negates the public statements?

HOLDING AND DECISION: (Newman, J.) Yes. A duty to disclose arises whenever secret information renders prior public statements materially misleading, not merely when that information completely negates the public statements. None of the statements made by Time Warner (D) constitutes an affirmative misrepresentation. However, the allegations of nondisclosure are more serious. Whether consideration of the alternative approach constitutes material information and whether its nondisclosure renders the original disclosure misleading remain questions for the trier of fact. An omission is actionable under the securities laws only when the corporation is subject to a duty to disclose the omitted facts. When, as here, a corporation pursuing a specific business goal announces an intended approach for reaching it, the corporation may be obligated to disclose other approaches which are under active and serious consideration. The allegations of nondisclosure and of a motive theory indicating scienter are sufficient to withstand a motion to dismiss. Reversed in part, affirmed in part, and remanded.

DISSENT: (Winter, J.) Neither Time Warner (D) nor its shareholders (P) profited from any delay in announcing the variable-price rights offering. The argument regarding a motive for such delay posits a scenario that is inconsistent with assumptions underlying securities law, statements in the complaint, and any plausible understanding of the operation of capital markets. Thus, dismissal of the complaint should be affirmed.

EDITOR'S ANALYSIS: Scienter is a necessary element of every Rule 10b-5 action. A plaintiff may plead scienter without direct knowledge of a defendant's state of mind by alleging facts establishing a motive to commit fraud and an opportunity to do so or by alleging facts constituting circumstantial evidence of either reckless or conscious behavior. In this case, the district court concluded that the complaint fell short under either approach. In the aftermath of any ruling that upholds the dismissal of a Rule 10b-5 suit, there will be some opportunity for unremedied fraud, while in the aftermath of any ruling that permits a Rule 10b-5 suit to progress beyond a motion to dismiss, there will be some opportunity to extract an undeserved settlement.

NOTES:

JORDAN v. DUFF & PHELPS, INC.
815 F.2d 429 (7th Cir. 1987), cert. denied, 485 U.S. 901 (1988).

NATURE OF CASE: Action for damages for fraud in a securities transaction.

FACT SUMMARY: Jordan (P), an employee of Duff & Phelps (D), sold his stock back to the company pursuant to his resignation shortly before a merger made the stock much more valuable.

CONCISE RULE OF LAW: Close corporations may not buy their own stock from employees without informing them of new events that substantially affect the value of the stock.

FACTS: Jordan (P) was employed as a securities analyst for Duff & Phelps (D) from May 1977 to December 1983. In 1981, Duff & Phelps (D) offered Jordan (P) the opportunity to buy stock in the company, and Jordan (P) purchased 188 shares and began making installment payments on another sixty-two shares. Jordan (P) purchased the stock at book value and was required to sign an agreement that required him to sell the stock back to the company upon any termination of his employment with Duff & Phelps (D). Under the agreement, Jordan (P) would be paid the adjusted book value of the stock at the end of the year prior to termination. Subsequently, Duff & Phelps (D) adopted a resolution that allowed employees who were fired to keep their stock for five years. Jordan (P) was forced to look for another job outside the area due to personal problems and accepted employment from another company in late 1983. Meanwhile, Duff & Phelps (D) was negotiating the sale of the firm for an amount that would greatly increase the value of the shares. When Jordan (P) informed Duff & Phelps (D) that he was planning on resigning, he was not told anything about the merger negotiations but was allowed to work until the end of 1983 so that the adjusted book value of his shares would reflect the 1983 earnings. Jordan's (P) resignation was effective on December 31, 1983, and he was given $23,225 for his shares of stock. On January 10, 1984, Duff & Phelps (D) was bought by Security Pacific, and, under the terms of the merger, Jordan's (P) stock would have been worth approximately $452,000. Jordan (P) filed suit, asserting damages measured by the difference in price.

ISSUE: Must close corporations disclose information that substantially affects the value of stock before buying the stock from an employee?

HOLDING AND DECISION: (Easterbrook, J.) Yes. Close corporations may not buy their own stock from employees without informing them of new events that substantially affect the value of the stock. Corporate law provides for a fiduciary duty running from knowledgeable insiders of closely held companies who buy stock from outsiders, such as employees. Under this duty, insiders must disclose material facts to outsiders in securities transactions. This duty may be altered by contract. Therefore, closely held corporations may contract with employees to allow for no duty of disclosure in stock transactions. This type of arrangement would uncouple the investment decision from the employment decision. Jordan (P) was an employee at will who did not sign a contract with Duff & Phelps (D). The course of dealing between Jordan (P) and Duff & Phelps (D) suggests that the firm did not demand that employees make employment decisions without regard to the value of the stock they owned in the company. Thus, Duff & Phelps (D) did not contractually alter its fiduciary duty to disclose material facts in the purchase of Jordan's (P) stock. The impending takeover by Security Pacific was a material fact that Duff & Phelps (D) withheld from Jordan (P). Therefore, Duff & Phelps (D) breached its fiduciary duty and is liable for damages to Jordan (P).

DISSENT: (Posner, J.) The mere existence of a fiduciary relationship between a corporation and its shareholders does not require a duty of disclosure of material information. The stock purchase agreement that Jordan (P) signed is incompatible with an inference that Duff & Phelps (D) undertook a duty to keep him abreast of developments affecting the value of his shares.

EDITOR'S ANALYSIS: Involuntary termination may lead to a different result. One court has determined that, where the death of the shareholder employee triggers the sell-back provision, there is no duty to disclose material information by the company. In St. Louis Union Trust Co. v. Merrill Lynch, Pierce, Fenner & Smith, 562 F.2d 1040 (8th Cir. 1977), the court reasoned that the shareholder was not making an "investment decision" where there was no control over the triggering event.

NOTES:

COWIN v. BRESLER
741 F.2d 410 (D.C. Cir. 1984).

NATURE OF CASE: Appeal from the dismissal of a suit seeking an injunction under Rule 10b-5.

FACT SUMMARY: Cowin (P), a shareholder of Bresler & Reiner, Inc. (D), sought an injunction under Rule 10b-5 to prevent misleading statements by the company.

CONCISE RULE OF LAW: Standing under § 10(b) of the Securities Exchange Act of 1934 and Rule 10b-5 is limited to purchasers and sellers of securities.

FACTS: Bresler & Reiner (D), a publicly owned company, engaged in the development of residential and commercial properties. Cowin (P), a minority shareholder, sued Bresler (D) and its directors (D), who owned 79% of Bresler (D). Cowin (P) alleged that the directors (D) manipulated the business for profit at the expense of the minority shareholders by disseminating reports to public shareholders that were materially deceptive. Cowin (P) alleged that the directors (D) eliminated the public market for the stock through their deceptions and brought the suit for an injunction under § 10(b) of the Securities Exchange Act of 1934 and Rule 10b-5. Bresler (D) responded that Cowin (P) did not have standing because he was not a purchaser or seller of stock. The trial court dismissed the injunction claim, and Cowin (P) appealed.

ISSUE: Is standing under § 10(b) of the Securities Exchange Act of 1934 and Rule 10b-5 limited to purchasers and sellers of securities?

HOLDING AND DECISION: (Bork, J.) Yes. Standing under § 10(b) of the Securities Exchange Act of 1934 and Rule 10b-5 is limited to purchasers and sellers of securities. The Supreme Court ruled in Blue Chip Stamps v. Manor Drug Stores, 421 U.S. 723 (1975), that only sellers or purchasers can pursue a claim for damages under Rule 10b-5. The scope of §10(b) and Rule 10b-5 is limited to fraud in connection with the purchase or sale of a security. Thus, the seller-purchaser limitation is supported by the language of the Securities Exchange Act. It would be inappropriate to relax this standing requirement for plaintiffs who seek injunctive relief because a flat rule remains consistent with the policy considerations of the Act. Furthermore, the Blue Chip decision expressly acknowledged that shareholders who have suffered loss in value due to fraudulent insider activity were barred from bringing 10b-5 actions. Therefore, plaintiffs bringing actions for damages or injunctions under Rule 10b-5 must have standing as a purchaser or seller. Cowin (P) did not buy or sell any shares of Bresler (D) and falls directly within the group acknowledged in Blue Chip prior to his suit for injunctive relief. Thus, Cowin (P) does not have standing under §10(b) and Rule 10b-5. Affirmed.

EDITOR'S ANALYSIS: Prior to the Blue Chip case, an exception to the general rule of standing under Rule 10b-5 was recognized in Mutual Shares Corp. v. Genesco, 384 F.2d 540 (2nd Cir. 1967). That court granted standing to current shareholders who sought an injunction under Rule 10b-5. Some courts have continued to recognize this exception even after Blue Chip.

NOTES:

HUDDLESTON v. HERMAN & MACLEAN
640 F.2d 534 (5th Cir. 1981), affd. on other grounds, 459 U.S. 683 (1983).

NATURE OF CASE: Appeal from an award of damages for violations of Rule 10b-5.

FACT SUMMARY: Huddleston (P), a purchaser of TIS stock, sued Herman & MacLean (D), the accounting firm that participated in the offering and registration statement, under Rule 10b-5.

CONCISE RULE OF LAW: In order to recover under Rule 10b-5, a plaintiff must show that reasonable reliance on a misrepresentation or omission caused the loss.

FACTS: In 1969, Texas International Speedway (TIS) filed a registration statement in connection with a public offering of securities. The proceeds were to be used to finance the construction of an automobile speedway. TIS filed for bankruptcy in 1970. Huddleston (P) filed a class action on behalf of purchasers of the securities sold by TIS against the participants in the offering, including Herman & MacLean (D), the accounting firm that had issued an opinion on the financial statements included in the registration under Rule 10b-5. The district court ruled for Huddleston (P) and the class at trial. Herman & MacLean (D) appealed, contending that Huddleston (P) had not proved reliance and causation.

ISSUE: Must a plaintiff prove that reasonable reliance on a material misrepresentation or omission caused the loss under Rule 10b-5?

HOLDING AND DECISION: (Rubin, J.) Yes. In order to recover under Rule 10b-5, a plaintiff must show that reasonable reliance on a misrepresentation or omission caused the loss. In the common law deceit action from which Rule 10b-5 was derived, it was necessary for the plaintiff to show reliance on the misrepresentations as a prerequisite to recovery. Thus, reliance is an issue in every Rule 10b-5 action. However, where nondisclosure of material information forms the basis for the complaint, proof of nonreliance becomes an affirmative defense because a presumption of reliance arises. This presumption only arises where the defendant stays silent in the face of duty to disclose. Where a defendant discloses information that is alleged to be misleading and omits facts that would make the information not misleading, the presumption of reliance does not arise. Plaintiffs under Rule 10b-5 must subjectively rely on the misrepresentations, and the reliance must be reasonable. Causation, a related subject, is also required under Rule 10b-5. Plaintiffs must prove that the misleading statements were also the proximate cause of the damages. Without this requirement, Rule 10b-5 would become an insurance plan for the cost of every security purchased in reliance on a material misstatement. The district court failed to submit both the reliance and causation questions to the jury in the case against Herman & MacLean (D). Therefore, the judgment is vacated. Reversed.

EDITOR'S ANALYSIS: Courts sometimes call reliance "transaction causation." In this context, the fraud must be the cause of the investment decision. "Loss causation" refers to the causal link between the fraud and the claimant's economic loss. Other courts have applied the presumption of reliance more liberally in circumstances such as those in the present case where material information is left out of a document or communication.

NOTES:

BASIC, INC. v. LEVINSON
485 U.S. 224 (1988).

NATURE OF CASE: Appeal from summary judgment in an action for violation of Rule 10b-5.

FACT SUMMARY: A class of shareholders (P) of Basic (D) contended that a presumption of reliance arose in their Rule 10b-5 action against Basic (D).

CONCISE RULE OF LAW: A rebuttable presumption of reliance is appropriate where misrepresentations have caused fraud-on-the-market under Rule 10b-5.

FACTS: In 1976, Combustion Engineering began to take steps to acquire Basic (D), a company that manufactured chemical refractories. Combustion officers met with Basic (D) officers and directors concerning the possibility of a merger. However, Basic (D) made three public statements, including a reply to an inquiry by the New York Stock Exchange, denying that it was involved in merger negotiations. On December 18, 1978, Basic (D) finally released a statement that it had been approached about a merger, and the next day the Basic (D) board endorsed Combustion's offer of $46 per share. Former shareholders (P) of Basic (D) who sold their stock after Basic's (D) first statement denying merger negotiations filed a class action for violations of Rule 10b-5, which bars false or misleading material statements in regard to securities trading. Basic (D) responded that shareholders (P) had not demonstrated reliance. The trial court applied a presumption of reliance but granted summary judgment to Basic (D) on other grounds. The court of appeals reversed, and Basic (D) appealed.

ISSUE: May a rebuttable presumption of reliance be applied to misrepresentations under a fraud-on-the-market theory?

HOLDING AND DECISION: (Blackmun, J.) Yes. A rebuttable presumption of reliance is appropriate where misrepresentations have caused fraud-on-the-market under Rule 10b-5. Reliance is an element of a Rule 10b-5 action because it provides the requisite causal connection between a defendant's misrepresentation and the injury. However, in cases where the duty to disclose material information has been breached, a presumption of reliance arises. Since the modern securities market differs from the face-to-face transactions contemplated by the early fraud cases, the reliance requirement must also be adjusted to account for these differences. When the market is interposed between the seller and buyer, the market price transmits information to the buyer. Congress assumed that the market price would reflect all publicly available information and hence, any material misrepresentations. Thus, purchasers on the market rely on the integrity of the market price. Therefore, where fraud alters the market price, a rebuttable presumption of reliance is also appropriate. This fraud-on-the-market presumption also overcomes the unrealistic evidentiary burden that a class action under Rule 10b-5 would face. The defendant may still rebut the presumption by showing that the misrepresentations did not alter the market price or that an individual purchaser would still have traded despite knowledge of the fraud.

DISSENT IN PART: (White, J.) Investors do not rely on the integrity of the market price because this implies that stock has true value measurable apart from the market price. Even if securities had a distinct, knowable value, investors do not always share the presumption that a stock's price reflects this value. In fact, most investors purchase or sell stock because they believe that the price does not reflect the true value.

EDITOR'S ANALYSIS: Other courts have allowed recovery under a presumption of reliance even where the investor purchased the stock without regard to its market price. In Panzirer v. Wolf, 663 F.2d 365 (2nd Cir. 1981), a woman who bought securities because of an article she read touting one of the company's products was allowed to recover, although the material misstatements regarding earnings were unrelated to the product.

NOTES:

ROWE v. MAREMONT CORP.
850 F.2d 1226 (7th Cir. 1988).

NATURE OF CASE: Appeal of an award of damages in action for securities fraud.

FACT SUMMARY: Rowe (P), who was defrauded by Maremont (D) in a stock transaction, sought an award of damages representing the amount that Maremont (D) profited in a subsequent sale of the securities.

CONCISE RULE OF LAW: Under Rule 10b-5, defrauded sellers are entitled to the difference between the fair value of what was received and the fair value of what would have been received if there had been no fraudulent conduct.

FACTS: Rowe (P) owned 9,000 shares of Pemcor. In 1977, Rowe (P) negotiated with Maremont (D) for the sale of the stock. During negotiations, Rowe (P) inquired about Maremont's (D) intentions regarding a tender offer for Pemcor stock. Maremont (D) assured Rowe (P) that there were no plans, but shortly after Rowe (P) sold the shares to Maremont (D), a tender offer was commenced. As a result, Pemcor arranged a merger with a third party, and Maremont (D) made a profit of $4 million in the transaction from the shares purchased by Rowe (P). Rowe (P) filed suit for securities fraud under Rule 10b-5 and prevailed on the liability issue. The trial court awarded Rowe (P) $745,423 in damages. Both parties appealed the award.

ISSUE: Are defrauded sellers entitled to the difference between the fair value of what was received and the fair value of what would have been received if there had been no fraudulent conduct under Rule 10b-5?

HOLDING AND DECISION: (Manion, J.) Yes. Under Rule 10b-5, defrauded sellers are entitled to the difference between the fair value of what was received and the fair value of what would have been received if there had been no fraudulent conduct. The Supreme Court has ruled in Affiliated Ute Citizens of Utah v. United States, 406 U.S. 128 (1972), that, in situations where the defendant received more than the seller's actual loss, the damages are the amount of the defendant's profit. However, despite this broad language, the disgorgement of profits is a rescissionary measure that is meant to place a defrauded seller in the same position as he would have occupied had there been no fraud. Disgorgement prevents a defendant from being unjustly enriched by the fraud but is not punitive. However, in situations where the seller would have sold the securities despite the fraud, the correct measure of damages is the difference in fair market value since this places the seller in the same position as he would have occupied absent the fraud. In this case, Rowe (P) would have sold the shares of stock to Maremont (D) even if he had known of the planned tender offer, although he would have negotiated for a higher price. Therefore, the correct measure of damages is the difference between the price paid and the fair value of the stock had Rowe (P) known the truth. The district court's determination that the fair value of Rowe's (P) Pemcor stock would have been 25% higher was reasonable. Affirmed.

EDITOR'S ANALYSIS: This decision represents the most common standard for damages under Rule 10b-5. The out-of-pocket measure is based upon the difference in the amount paid and the actual value at the time of the transaction. Thus, events taking place after the transaction do not affect the value, and unjust enrichment considerations often appear. Courts have difficulty in determining fair value since there are many extraneous factors affecting the market price of stock.

NOTES:

Notes

CHAPTER 12
THE REGULATION OF INSIDER TRADING

QUICK REFERENCE RULES OF LAW

1. **The Source of a Duty to Abstain or Disclose.** Under § 10(b) of the Securities Exchange Act, a duty to disclose does not arise from the mere possession of nonpublic information. (Chiarella v. United States)

2. **Tippers and Tippees.** A "tippee" does not violate securities laws by trading on inside information if his sources did not reveal the information for personal gain. (Dirks v. SEC)

3. **The Misappropriation Theory.** An employee's misappropriation of confidential information provides the basis for fraud under Rule 10b-5. (United States v. Carpenter)

4. **The Misappropriation Theory.** Criminal liability under Rule 10b-5 cannot be predicated upon the mere misappropriation of information in breach of a fiduciary duty owed to one who is neither a purchaser nor seller of securities. (United States v. Bryan)

5. **The Scope of Section 16(b).** A corporate insider must have realized direct pecuniary benefit to have violated § 16(b) of the Securities Exchange Act. (CBI Industries v. Horton)

6. **Unorthodox Transactions: The Takeover Problem.** Traditional cash-for-stock sales within the context of a takeover may form the basis for § 16(b) liability. (Texas International Airlines v. National Airlines, Inc.)

CHIARELLA v. UNITED STATES
445 U.S. 222 (1980).

NATURE OF CASE: Appeal from a conviction for securities fraud.

FACT SUMMARY: Chiarella (D), an employee at a financial printing business, deduced the names of target companies prior to the public announcements of takeover bids and used the information to make profits in the stock market.

CONCISE RULE OF LAW: Under § 10(b) of the Securities Exchange Act, a duty to disclose does not arise from the mere possession of nonpublic information.

FACTS: Chiarella (D) worked for Pandick Press, a financial printer, from 1975 to 1976. Chiarella (D) handled documents that announced corporate takeover bids. Although the identities of the companies were concealed on the documents, Chiarella (D) was able to deduce the names of the target companies. He then purchased stock in those companies before the takeover bids were announced, sold the shares after the announcement, and made $30,000 in profit over fourteen months. The Federal Government (P) charged Chiarella (D) with securities fraud under § 10(b) of the Securities Exchange Act. Chiarella (D) was convicted, and he appealed.

ISSUE: Does a duty to disclose arise from the mere possession of nonpublic information under § 10(b) of the Securities Exchange Act?

HOLDING AND DECISION: (Powell, J.) No. Under § 10(b) of the Securities Exchange Act, a duty to disclose does not arise from the mere possession of nonpublic information. Silence in connection with the purchase or sale of securities may operate as actionable fraud under §10(b) under certain circumstances. This liability is premised upon a duty to disclose arising from a relationship of trust between the parties to the transaction. This duty to disclose guarantees that corporate insiders will not benefit through fraudulent use of nonpublic information. However, the language of §10(b) does not support a general duty between all participants in the market to disclose all material, nonpublic information. Chiarella (D) had no relationship with the sellers of the target company's securities that he purchased. Chiarella (D) was not an agent or a fiduciary; he was a complete stranger who dealt with the sellers only through the market. Thus, Chiarella (D) had no duty under §10(b) to disclose the information he had. Therefore, Chiarella's conviction must be overturned.

DISSENT: (Blackmun, J.) The majority's approach unduly minimizes the importance of Chiarella's (D) access to confidential information that honest investors could not legally obtain. The common law of actionable misrepresentation treats the possession of special facts as a key ingredient in the duty to disclose.

EDITOR'S ANALYSIS: A concurring opinion by Justice Stevens and a dissenting opinion by Chief Justice Burger suggested that some version of a misappropriation theory could still form the basis for a conviction. However, this type of theory was not properly pleaded in Chiarella's (D) original trial, according to a majority of the Court. This decision is important because it implied for the first time that insiders do owe an affirmative duty of disclosure.

NOTES:

DIRKS v. SEC
463 U.S. 646 (1983).

NATURE OF CASE: Review of administrative censure.

FACT SUMMARY: Dirks (D), a "tippee," gave investment advice based on inside information which had been obtained from tippers not acting for personal gain.

CONCISE RULE OF LAW: A "tippee" does not violate securities laws by trading on inside information if his sources did not reveal the information for personal gain.

FACTS: Dirks (D), a stock market analyst, became aware of allegations that Equity Funding of America was in precarious financial condition due to massive fraud. He undertook an investigation. Based on information obtained from certain insiders, Dirks (D) concluded that Equity Funding was in weak financial shape and that its value would greatly diminish when the facts became known. He advised several clients to sell. Subsequently, Equity Funding's situation became known to the pubic and its value plummeted. The SEC (P) undertook an investigation resulting in Dirks' (D) being held by the SEC (P) to have violated Rule 10b-5 by trading on inside information. As punishment, he was censured. The Court of Appeals for the District of Columbia affirmed, and the U.S. Supreme Court granted review.

ISSUE: Does a "tippee" violate securities laws by trading on inside information if his sources did not reveal the information for personal gain?

HOLDING AND DECISION: (Powell, J.) No. A "tippee" does not violate securities laws by trading on inside information if his sources did not reveal the information for personal gain. Securities laws do not exist to guarantee equal access to information for all investors. They exist to prevent those having access to inside information from using their privileged positions for personal gain. Consequently, one who is not an insider cannot, as a usual matter, violate Rule 10b-5 for using inside information, as there is no violation of a position of trust in doing so. The exception to this rule is when the tipper/insider uses the tippee as a conduit for trading on his own behalf. This will occur when the tipper realizes some personal benefit by providing the information in question. Here, Dirks (D) was not an insider. There was no evidence that his sources received any benefit by providing him with information regarding Equity Funding. This being so, Dirks (D) did not violate Rule 10b-5. Reversed.

DISSENT: (Blackmun, J.) Where a tippee's source is a fiduciary, the tippee may not trade on inside information any more than could the fiduciary.

EDITOR'S ANALYSIS: This case was a logical followup to Chiarella v. United States, 445 U.S. 222 (1980). In that case, Chiarelia, an employee of a printer of financial documents, discovered an impending transaction due to the fact he was printing memorialization documents. He traded on the information. The Court held that Chiarella had not violated Rule 10b-5 because he was not a fiduciary.

NOTES:

UNITED STATES v. CARPENTER
791 F.2d 1024 (2d. Cir. 1986).

NATURE OF CASE: Appeal from a conviction for aiding and abetting securities fraud.

FACT SUMMARY: Carpenter (D) and Winans (D), employees of the Wall Street Journal, participated in a scheme whereby securities were traded on the basis of articles that were to appear in the Journal.

CONCISE RULE OF LAW: An employee's misappropriation of confidential information provides the basis for fraud under Rule 10b-5.

FACTS: In 1981, Winans (D) was a reporter for the Wall Street Journal and one of the writers of the "Heard on the Street" column. This column was widely read and very influential in the stock market. Carpenter (D) was a news clerk at the Journal. Company policy deemed all information acquired by employees during the course of their employment to be confidential and the property of the Journal. Winans (D) and Carpenter (D) participated in a scheme whereby they relayed advance information on the content of the "Heard" column to brokers who would trade the subject securities. In 1983 and 1984, Winans (D) and Carpenter (D) made prepublication trades on the basis of advance knowledge of approximately twenty-seven "Heard" columns. The net profit from the scheme was close to $690,000. Winans (D) did not alter journalistic content of the column during the scheme. The SEC discovered the plan and charged Winans (D) and Carpenter (D) with securities fraud. Following their convictions, Winans (D) and Carpenter (D) appealed.

ISSUE: Does an employee's misappropriation of confidential information provide the basis for fraud under Rule 10b-5?

HOLDING AND DECISION: (Pierce, J.) Yes. An employee's misappropriation of confidential information provides the basis for fraud under Rule 10b-5. Section 10(b) of the Securities Exchange Act broadly proscribes deceptive practices in connection with the purchase or sale of securities. However, merely using information not available to others does not give rise to a violation of Rule 10b-5. There must be a breach of a duty to disclose or a breach of a duty of confidentiality owed to an employer. An employer may insist on a duty of confidentiality regarding information acquired during employment in order to maintain its reputation. Theft of valuable confidential information from an employer is equivalent to stealing nonpublic information from traditional corporate insiders. Winans (D) and Carpenter (D) misappropriated information regarding the schedule of forthcoming publications from the Journal. This breached their duty of confidentiality. This constituted a fraud upon the Journal because it damaged its reputation. Furthermore, those who purchased or bought the securities at issue would not have traded at the transaction price had they known about the information used by Winans (D) and Carpenter (D). Therefore, Winans (D) and Carpenter (D) have committed fraud in connection with securities transactions, which is prohibited by Rule 10b-5. Affirmed.

EDITOR'S ANALYSIS: The court rejected the defendant's argument that they could not be held liable for acts which the Journal could legally commit. The court held that although the Journal could destroy its own reputation by making prepublication trades, employees did not have the right to misappropriate their informational property. The Supreme Court granted certiorari in this case but deadlocked 4–4. The convictions were affirmed on the basis of mail fraud, but the federal securities issue remains open.

NOTES:

UNITED STATES v. BRYAN
58 F.3d 933 (4th Cir. 1995).

NATURE OF CASE: Review of federal convictions under wire and mail fraud, and securities violations.

FACT SUMMARY: Bryan (D) purchased stock in companies which sold video gaming equipment, knowing through his position as Lottery Director that the state was planning to expand into that area of gambling.

CONCISE RULE OF LAW: Criminal liability under Rule 10b-5 cannot be predicated upon the mere misappropriation of information in breach of a fiduciary duty owed to one who is neither a purchaser nor seller of securities.

FACTS: Bryan (D) was the Director of the West Virginia State Lottery. In his position he became aware of state plans to move into the video gambling business. Certain planned contracts, in conjunction with the video gaming program, were to substantially enhance the financial picture for the companies involved. Bryan (D) purchased stocks based upon his knowledge of the contracts that were going to be awarded to video gaming equipment manufacturers. Bryan (D) was convicted for mail and wire fraud, and for securities violations under Rule 10b-5. The Fourth Circuit affirmed the mail and wire fraud convictions. The court then turned to the question of the securities conviction.

ISSUE: Can criminal liability be predicated on a misappropriation theory violation of Rule 10b-5?

HOLDING AND DECISION: (Luttig, J.) No. Criminal liability under Rule 10b-5 cannot be predicated upon the mere misappropriation of information in breach of a fiduciary duty owed to one who is neither a purchaser nor seller of securities. The Supreme Court has specified that the primary factor motivating securities regulations is the protection of market certainty and predictability. The original purpose of the regulations was to prevent a buyer or seller of securities from being deceived in conjunction with the transaction. The Supreme Court has said that a general theory of fraud-on-the-market is insupportable. Furthermore, the patchwork quilt of decisions based upon misappropriation theory analysis of Rule 10b-5 has only served to cloud the market. Investors no longer have certainty as to what actions are proscribed and which are not. In this case, Bryan (D) clearly acted scurilously. However, Section 10(b) is not the appropriate vehicle through which to control his actions. Trading on improperly obtained information is unfair. However, Bryan (D) did not perpetrate a fraud on a purchaser or seller of the securities. Thus, his conduct does not fit Rule 10b-5. Reversed.

EDITOR'S ANALYSIS: The Supreme Court has reserved the right to consider at some later date whether the aquisition of nonpublic information creates a duty to disclose. Such an approach might be more workable than the current fraud on the source method. Newer congressional legislation appears to favor this approach, as was evidenced by their creation of a private misappropriation of information cause of action.

NOTES:

CBI INDUSTRIES v. HORTON
682 F.2d 643 (7th Cir. 1982).

NATURE OF CASE: Appeal of damage award in a suit to recover insider trading profits.

FACT SUMMARY: Horton (D), a director of CBI (P), sold CBI (P) shares on the open market and within six months bought CBI (P) shares, at a lower price, for his sons' trust fund.

CONCISE RULE OF LAW: A corporate insider must have realized direct pecuniary benefit to have violated § 16(b) of the Securities Exchange Act.

FACTS: Horton (D) was a director of CBI (P). He sold 3,000 shares of his CBI (P) stock on the open market. Within six months, Horton (D) bought 2,000 shares of the stock on the open market at a lower price than he had sold the 3,000 shares. The 2,000 shares were purchased for his sons' trust fund. CBI (P) sued Horton (D) for $25,000, the difference in price multiplied by 2,000. CBI (P) prevailed, and Horton (D) appealed.

ISSUE: Must a corporate insider have realized direct pecuniary benefit to have violated § 16(b) of the Securities Exchange Act?

HOLDING AND DECISION: (Posner, J.) Yes. A corporate insider must have realized direct pecuniary benefit to have violated § 16(b) of the Securities Exchange Act. A person may be just as tempted to use insider information to increase the wealth of his children as to increase his own. Limiting § 16(b) to personal pecuniary receipts seems to ignore human nature. However, the Congress of 1934 gave no indication that it intended to sweep so broadly. Applying the intended standards of Congress to this case, Horton (D) cannot be held liable for the monetization of any emotional benefits he received by increasing his sons' wealth. However, Horton (D) could be liable for the actuarially computed increase in his contingent remainder in his sons' trust; an expected value is a form of direct pecuniary benefit. Reversed and remanded.

EDITOR'S ANALYSIS: Judge Posner raises the issue of tension between evaluating a person's wealth in a realistic sense as opposed to a purely pecuniary sense. While it is true that some individuals might receive as much personal pleasure from using insider information to benefit, for example, their alma mater as they would in profiting themselves, it is a practical impossibility to know the emotional value of a trade to an insider. Personal monetary profit, on the other hand, is readily identifiable.

NOTES:

TEXAS INTERNATIONAL AIRLINES v. NATIONAL AIRLINES INC.
714 F.2d 533 (5th Cir. 1983).

NATURE OF CASE: Appeal from summary judgment in an action for declaratory relief and counterclaim for recovery of short-swing profits.

FACT SUMMARY: Texas International (TI) (P) sold its National (D) stock to Pan Am as part of a merger within the period of short-swing transactions covered by § 16(b).

CONCISE RULE OF LAW: Traditional cash-for-stock sales within the context of a takeover may form the basis for § 16(b) liability.

FACTS: In March 1979, TI (P) purchased 121,000 shares of National (D) common stock as part of an attempt to gain control of National (D). On the date of the purchase, TI (P) owned more than 10% of National (D). Approximately four months later, TI (P) and Pan American Airways entered into a stock purchase agreement whereby TI (P) agreed to sell 790,700 shares of National (D) stock to Pan Am at $50 a share. In 1978, National (D) and Pan Am had entered into a merger agreement that provided for an exchange of $50 for each share of National (D) stock. The merger agreement was to take effect in September 1979. Thus, TI (P), as a National (D) stockholder, would have received the same price for its stock under the merger agreement if it hadn't sold the National (D) stock in July 1979. Shortly after the sale, TI (P) sought declaratory relief that it was not liable to give the profits on 120,000 shares it purchased in March back to National (D). The trial court ruled for National (D), and TI (P) appealed.

ISSUE: May traditional cash-for-stock sales within the context of a takeover form the basis for § 16(b) liability?

HOLDING AND DECISION: (Johnson, J.) Yes. Traditional cash-for-stock sales within the context of a takeover may form the basis for § 16(b) liability. Section 16(b) imposes strict liability against insider traders who purchase and sell securities within a six-month period. Persons or companies that own more than 10% of a company's stock are considered insiders for purposes of §16(b). Congress intended that insiders should disgorge profits based upon access to confidential information. In Kern County Land Co. v. Occidental Petroleum Corp., 411 U.S. 582 (1973), the Supreme Court approved a narrow exception to §16(b) for unorthodox transactions such as hostile takeovers. In these transactions, the Court held that liability should only be imposed where there was access to confidential information. However, unorthodox transactions under Kern County do not include traditional cash-for-stock sales because these transactions are purely voluntary. Here, TI (P) voluntarily entered into the transaction with Pan Am before the merger was complete. The volitional character of the deal means that it does not fit the exception of Kern County and is sufficient reason to trigger the applicability of §16(b). Since TI (P) sold National (D) stock within six months of its purchase and owned more than 10% of the company, it may not keep the profits from the purchase under §16(b). Affirmed.

EDITOR'S ANALYSIS: Courts have had a lot of difficulty applying the Kern County exception articulated by the Supreme Court. Some courts have agreed with this decision, while others have ruled that some voluntary transactions are unorthodox for purposes of the exception. See Pay Less Drug Stores v. Jewel Cos., 579 F.Supp. 1396 (N.D. Cal. 1984).

NOTES:

Notes

CHAPTER 13
SHAREHOLDER VOTING AND GOING-PRIVATE TRANSACTIONS

QUICK REFERENCE RULES OF LAW

1. **Fraud in Uncontested Elections.** Negligence is the correct standard for liability under § 14(a) of the Securities Exchange Act. (Gould v. American-Hawaiian Steamship Co.)

2. **Fraud in Uncontested Elections.** Demonstrably false or misleading statements of opinion or belief in a proxy statement may be actionable under securities laws. (Virginia Bankshares, Inc. v. Sandberg)

3. **Going-Private Transaction.** Disclosure required under § 13(e) for going-private transactions must be detailed and complete. (In re Meyers Parking System, Inc.)

GOULD v. AMERICAN-HAWAIIAN STEAMSHIP CO.
535 F.2d 761 (3d Cir. 1976).

NATURE OF CASE: Appeal from a judgment in a class action for violation of § 14(a) of the Securities Exchange Act.

FACT SUMMARY: Casey (D), a director of McLean Industries (D), claimed that he was not liable for a misleading proxy solicitation under §14(a) since he acted in good faith.

CONCISE RULE OF LAW: Negligence is the correct standard for liability under § 14(a) of the Securities Exchange Act.

FACTS: Casey (D) was a director of McLean Industries (D). McLean (D) submitted a proxy solicitation regarding a proposed merger to the shareholders (P) that was materially deficient in violation of § 14(a) of the Securities Exchange Act and Rule 14a-9(a). The proxy statement falsely indicated that American-Hawaiian (D) and other entities had agreed to vote for the merger. A class action on behalf of the shareholders (P) was instituted against McLean (D) and all of its directors, including Casey (D). Casey (D) saw and approved the draft of the proxy statement but did not read the solicitation in its final form. The trial court held Casey (D) liable. Casey (D) appealed, responding that negligence was not the correct standard for liability under § 14(a).

ISSUE: Is negligence the correct standard for liability under § 14(a)?

HOLDING AND DECISION: (Maris, J.) Yes. Negligence is the correct standard for liability under § 14(a) of the Securities Exchange Act. Section 14 itself does not expressly indicate a standard for liability. Section 11 of the Securities Act of 1933, which deals with civil liability for false registration statements, is similar and analogous to § 14(a). Both sections proscribe false or misleading statements or omissions, and both enumerate specific classes of individuals who may be liable. Since § 11 clearly establishes negligence as the test for determining liability, the parallel between the sections strongly supports using negligence under § 14. The language of § 14(a) does not indicate that scienter is required, and the section is not similar to § 10(b), which prohibits deceptive practices in connection with the purchase and sale of securities. Furthermore, the broad remedial purpose of § 14(a) implies the need for a high standard of care. Therefore, given all these factors, the standard of due diligence and negligence is most appropriate for § 14(a). Casey (D) did not make any effort to correct the deficiencies in the proxy statement draft, nor did he read the final form of the solicitation. The district court's determination that this constituted negligence was reasonable. Affirmed.

EDITOR'S ANALYSIS: This decision is in accord with the majority rule. A minority of courts have required scienter in § 14(a) actions. See Adams v. Standard Knitting Mills, Inc., 623 F.2d 422 (6th Cir. 1980). The Gould court also rejected Casey's (D) argument that he should not be held liable for damages because he had not profited from the merger. The court noted that the negligent directors were joint tortfeasors who were jointly and severally liable for the entire damage, regardless of the benefit received.

NOTES:

VIRGINIA BANKSHARES, INC. v. SANDBERG
501 U.S. 1083, 111 S.Ct. 2749 (1991).

NATURE OF CASE: Appeal from verdict awarding damages for publishing a misleading proxy statement.

FACT SUMMARY: Sandberg (P) contended that a proxy statement that had contained expressions of opinion and belief had been misleading.

CONCISE RULE OF LAW: Demonstrably false or misleading statements of opinion or belief in a proxy statement may be actionable under securities laws.

FACTS: First American Bankshares, Inc. (FABI) (D) began a "freeze-out" merger in which it absorbed First American Bank of Virginia (Bank) (D) into Virginia Bankshares, Inc. (D), a wholly-owned subsidiary of FABI (D). An investment banking firm gave an opinion that the Bank's shares were worth $42 per share, which FABI's (D) directors ratified. A proxy statement was issued in which the directors urged approval of the merger at $42 per share because, they claimed, shareholders would achieve a "high" and "fair" price for their stock. Approval was effected. Sandberg (P), a shareholder who had opposed the merger, sued for damages. She contended that the shares had been worth $60 and that the proxy statement had therefore been misleading in violation of SEC Rule 14a-9. A jury awarded damages, which the court of appeals affirmed. Virginia Bankshares (D) appealed, contending that statements of opinion were not actionable as misstatements of material fact under Rule 14a-9.

ISSUE: May demonstrably false or misleading statements of opinion or belief in a proxy statement be actionable under securities laws?

HOLDING AND DECISION: (Souter, J.) Yes. Demonstrably false or misleading statements of opinion or belief in a proxy statement may be actionable under securities laws. Rule 14a-9 prohibits false or misleading statements of fact in a proxy statement. Virginia Bankshares (D) contends that FABI's (D) directors made only expressions of opinion, not facts, in their proxy statement, and that therefore the situation falls outside the ambit of the Rule. However, conclusory terms in a commercial context are reasonably understood by the investing public to be predicated on a factual basis. In this case, whether $42 was "high," and the proposal "fair," as the directors so stated, depends on whether provable facts exists to substantiate these conclusions. Consequently, if a plaintiff can prove that the facts underlying a statement of opinion in a proxy statement were an insufficient basis for such opinion, a Rule 14a-9 violation may be said to have occurred. In this case, there was evidence of a "going concern" value for the Bank (D) in excess of $60 per share, which FABI's (D) directors did not disclose. Affirmed.

EDITOR'S ANALYSIS: As the present case illustrates, courts do allow plaintiffs some leeway under the securities laws, as a technical reading of Rule 14a-9 would have supported the defendant's position. However, there are certainly limits on how speculative a claim can be. A good example is Blue Chip Stamps v. Manor Drug Stores, 421 U.S. 123 (1975). There, the Court said that one who elected not to invest due to a misleading statement had no cause of action, since how he actually would have invested could not be proven.

NOTES:

IN RE MEYERS PARKING SYSTEM, INC.
Exchange Act. Rel. No. 26,069 (1988).

NATURE OF CASE: SEC determination on alleged violation of § 13(e) of the Securities Exchange Act.

FACT SUMMARY: Fink-Gordon (D) sought to buy out the minority shareholders of Meyers Parking System (MPS) and filed the required statements under §13(e).

CONCISE RULE OF LAW: Disclosure required under § 13(e) for going-private transactions must be detailed and complete.

FACTS: Fink-Gordon (D) proposed a buy-out merger of the minority shareholders of Meyers Parking System (MPS). By the terms of the merger, the minority shareholders, who owned 20% of the stock, were to be paid $22 a share. The day after the merger was announced, the price rose from $17.50 to $25 a share on the market. Following the announcement of the going-private transaction, five separate groups of shareholders filed actions against Fink-Gordon (D) and their subsidiary, the MPS Acquisition Corp. (D). These actions were consolidated, and an independent investment company was retained to evaluate the fairness of the merger. Shortly thereafter, MPS filed a Schedule 13E-3 containing a preliminary proxy statement regarding the proposed merger. The independent investment company advised Fink-Gordon (D) that a higher price for the shares was warranted and negotiated a price of $29.50 per share. MPS then filed a revised Schedule 13E-3 and later made other amendments. These materials provided little additional disclosure. The SEC (P) was asked to determine whether these filings were adequate.

ISSUE: Must disclosures required under § 13(e) for going-private transactions be detailed and complete?

HOLDING AND DECISION: Yes. Disclosure required under § 13(e) for going-private transactions must be detailed and complete. Schedule 13E-3 requires in Item 7(a) that the filing company state the purpose for the going-private transaction. Conclusory statements are not sufficient. Fink-Gordon's (D) filing stated only that the purpose of the transaction was to enable Fink-Gordon (D) to acquire the entire equity interest in MPS. This response is inadequate because it does not state the purpose. Item 7(d) must include a reasonably detailed discussion of the benefits and detriments of the going-private transaction to the parties. Other than a brief discussion of tax consequences, Fink-Gordon (D) did not give such a response in its filing. Item 8 requires various disclosure concerning the fairness of the transaction and the factors used to make a valuation of the stock. Fink-Gordon's (D) Schedule 13E-3 filing provided the conclusions of the independent investment company, but gave no detail as to the steps taken or the actual values calculated by the independent adviser. This type of response is inadequate. Accordingly, since the Schedule 13E-3 documents filed by Fink-Gordon (D) with regard to the going-private transaction involving MPS were not complete and detailed, the SEC (P) finds that Fink-Gordon (D) failed to comply with § 13(e) of the Securities Exchange Act.

EDITOR'S ANALYSIS: The SEC (P) also determined that Fink-Gordon's (D) responses to Items 3(b) and 9(a) on Schedule 13E-3 were insufficient. These items require the disclosure of any contacts or negotiations concerning potential mergers and reports or appraisals from outside parties relating to the going-private transaction. Most courts have found that § 13(e) provides a private right of action. See Howing v. Nationwide Corp., 826 F.2d 1470 (6th Cir. 1986).

NOTES:

CHAPTER 14
CORPORATE TAKEOVERS

QUICK REFERENCE RULES OF LAW

1. **The Early Warning System: Section 13(d).** A "group," for purposes of § 13(d) disclosure, includes an aggregation of members combined in furtherance of a common objective. (Wellman v. Dickinson)

2. **Disclosure Content.** Active adviser-brokers who have a history of close association and equity sharing with a takeover participant are "bidders" for purposes of § 14(d) disclosure. (MAI Basic Four, Inc. v. Prime Computer, Inc.)

3. **The All-Holders/Best-Price Rule.** If a stock transaction is an integral part of a tender offer, and the consideration paid for the stock is different than that in the tender offer, then the transaction violates Rule 14d-10. (Epstein v. MCA Corp.)

4. **"Tender Offer."** A stock repurchase offer made in response to a tender offer is not necessarily covered by tender offer rules. (SEC v. Carter Hawley Hale Stores, Inc.)

5. **Disclosure and Enforcement.** An element of a cause of action under § 14(e) of the Securities Exchange Act is misrepresentation or nondisclosure. (Schreiber v. Burlington Northern, Inc.)

6. **State Takeover Legislation.** The Williams Act does not preempt state antitakeover legislation that places investors on an equal footing with the takeover bidder. (CTS Corp. v. Dynamics Corp. of America)

WELLMAN v. DICKINSON
682 F.2d 355 (2d Cir. 1982), cert. denied, 460 U.S. 1069 (1983)

NATURE OF CASE: Appeal from judgment in an enforcement and private action under § 13(d) of the Securities Exchange Act.

FACT SUMMARY: Dickinson (D) contacted persons who had the power to dispose of Becton (P) stock and represented to potential purchasers that these persons and Dickinson (D) would make their shares readily available as a group but did not file documents under § 13(d).

CONCISE RULE OF LAW: A "group," for purposes of § 13(d) disclosure, includes an aggregation of members combined in furtherance of a common objective.

FACTS: Fairleigh Dickinson, Jr. (D) was a major stockholder in Becton (P) and owned 4.2% of the outstanding stock, as well as being a cotrustee of another large block. Dickinson (D) was Chairman of the Board of Becton (P) until 1977, when a bitter internal power struggle began and the Board voted to remove him. Dickinson (D) met with Salomon Brothers to obtain advice on how to regain control of Becton (P). It was decided that Dickinson (D) would attempt to find a company who would be willing to purchase Becton (P) stock, including Dickinson's (D) own shares, in order to take over the company. Dickinson (D) contacted persons who owned or had the power to dispose of significant blocks of Becton (P) stock but did not have voting control. Meanwhile, Salomon made presentations to potential buyers and represented that a large block of stock was available, including the contacts which Dickinson (D) had made. Potential takeover companies were assured that approximately 13% of the shares were readily available. Eventually, Sun Company became interested in the takeover. Becton's (P) management wished to remain independent and filed an action against Dickinson (D), claiming that he had joined a group holding ownership of 13% of the shares and had failed to disclose this fact as required under § 13(d). The SEC also filed an enforcement action that was joined at trial. The trial court ruled against Dickinson (D), who appealed.

ISSUE: Does a "group," for purposes of § 13(d) disclosure, include an aggregation of members combined in furtherance of a common objective?

HOLDING AND DECISION: (Moore, J.) Yes. A "group," for purposes of § 13(d) disclosure, includes an aggregation of members combined in furtherance of a common objective. Section 13(d) of the Securities Exchange Act requires that groups becoming the owner of more than 5% of the outstanding shares in a publicly held company must file a statement with the SEC. The statement must contain the identity of the acquirer, the number of shares owned, and the source of the funds. A "group" is defined as an aggregation of persons or entities who act for the purpose of acquiring, holding, or disposing securities. Thus, the members must combine in furtherance of a common objective. A common understanding among persons may be shown by evidence of representations made to third parties. Moreover, voting control is not the sole indication of beneficial ownership under § 13(d). The power to dispose of securities is a sufficient interest for purposes of a Schedule 13D filing. Dickinson's (D) representatives informed potential takeover participants that there was an understanding among the group of people contacted by Dickinson (D) that they were going to act as a group in selling their shares. The trial court could reasonably infer that these were assurances, and not predictions, by the group. Dickinson (D) and the others were linked by a desire to profit from a shift in the corporate control of Becton (P). Thus, they were an aggregation of persons with a common objective. Therefore, Dickinson (D) was required under § 13(d) to file documents indicating the group's power over 13% of the outstanding shares. Affirmed.

DISSENT: (Van Graafeiland, J.) Many of the persons whom Dickinson (D) contacted indicated that they did not have the power to assure a sale. Since there was no binding commitment by these parties, there was no aggregation for a common objective.

EDITOR'S ANALYSIS: Section 13(d) also requires that acquiring groups or parties disclose their intent with regard to the acquisition. A party who is considering a takeover attempt must disclose this fact even if the plan is far from certain. See K-N Energy, Inc. v. Gulf Interstate Corp., 607 F.Supp. 756 (D. Colo. 1983).

NOTES:

MAI BASIC FOUR INC. v. PRIME COMPUTER INC.
871 F.2d 212 (1st Cir. 1989).

NATURE OF CASE: Appeal from an injunction in an action for violations of § 14(d) of the Securities Exchange Act.

FACT SUMMARY: Prime Computer (D) alleged that MAI Basic Four (Basic) (P) failed to disclose the interest of Drexel Burnham Lambert, Basic's (P) investment adviser, in its attempted takeover of Prime (D).

CONCISE RULE OF LAW: Active adviser-brokers who have a history of close association and equity sharing with a takeover participant are "bidders" for purposes of § 14(d) disclosure.

FACTS: Basic (P) made a tender offer of $20 per share for all shares of Prime Computer (D) in 1989. The offer was conditioned upon a tender of 67% of the outstanding shares. The financing consisted of a small amount of cash and a large amount of high-yield, interest-bearing, increasing-rate notes commonly known as junk bonds. These junk bonds were to be sold by Drexel Burnham Lambert. Drexel was closely associated with Basic (D) and owned a 5% interest in the company with a right to purchase at half price another 9%. Drexel's role in placing the junk bonds would generate $65 million in fees if successful. Drexel anticipated furnishing any funds needed to complete the transaction if the notes were not completely sold. Basic (P) filed a complaint challenging state antitakeover statutes, and Prime (D) filed a counterclaim against Basic (P) for failing to disclose Drexel's involvement in the tender offer in the SEC filing as required by § 14(d). The trial court granted Prime (D) an injunction against consummation of the tender offer, and Basic (P) appealed.

ISSUE: Are active adviser-brokers who have a history of close association and equity sharing with a takeover participant "bidders" for purposes of § 14(d) disclosure?

HOLDING AND DECISION: (Coffin, J.) Yes. Active adviser-brokers who have a history of close association and equity sharing with a takeover participant are "bidders" for purposes of § 14(d) disclosure. Section 14(d) of the Securities Exchange Act prohibits a takeover unless the bidding company first files and transmits to the target company a form describing the identity of the bidder and the source of financing and purpose of the tender offer. Rule 14d-1 defines a "bidder" as any person who makes a tender offer or on whose behalf an offer is made. The SEC has asserted that "principal participants" in tender offers must be disclosed under this rule. Although some courts have adopted a bright-line approach excluding entities that will not control the target company, the language of the rule does not support such a narrow construction. Drexel was an active adviser-broker-financier-participant in the Basic (P) takeover bid. Although Drexel had only a 14% direct interest, its backing of the tender offer might be the indispensable key to its success. Therefore, it is a participant for the purposes of §14(d) filings. Thus, Basic (P) should have included information about Drexel in its filing documents. Affirmed.

EDITOR'S ANALYSIS: The court also noted that the information about Drexel was material because the financial strength or vulnerability of Drexel was critical to Prime (P) shareholders' consideration of the tender offer. Some courts have indicated that bidders must disclose all material information related to a tender offer. See Flynn v. Bass Bros. Enters. Inc., 744 F.2d 978 (3d. Cir. 1984).

NOTES:

EPSTEIN v. MCA CORP.
50 F.3d 644 (9th Cir. 1995).

NATURE OF CASE: Appeal of a shareholder suit claiming Rule 14d-10 violations during a tender offer.

FACT SUMMARY: Wasserman, an MCA insider, committed his shares to Matsushita (D) during a buyout, but his commitment was contingent on a successful tender offer, and the consideration Matsushita (D) paid him was higher than the tender offer price.

CONCISE RULE OF LAW: If a stock transaction is an integral part of a tender offer, and the consideration paid for the stock is different than that in the tender offer, then the transaction violates Rule 14d-10.

FACTS: Matsushita (D) sought to acquire MCA Corp. (D) in a tender offer. Matsushita (D) wanted Wasserman, an MCA (D) insider, to commit his shares to Matsushita (D) in advance, in part to keep him on as an employee after the change in ownership of MCA (D). An agreement was created whereby Wasserman would exchange his shares after the tender offer closed. In consideration for the commitment, Wasserman was to receive shares in a holding company; the value of the shares was linked to the tender offer price by a formula ensuring that the value would be greater than the tender offer price. If the tender offer went unsatisfied, the whole agreement between Wasserman and Matsushita (D) would dissolve. Former shareholders of MCA (P) filed suit, claiming discrimination in a tender offer in violation of Rule 14d-10. The case was subsequently appealed.

ISSUE: Can a stock transaction violate the Rule 14d-10 prohibition against special consideration paid during a tender offer if the transaction is an integral part of a tender offer and the consideration paid different than that in the tender offer?

HOLDING AND DECISION: (Per curiam) Yes. If a stock transaction is an integral part of a tender offer, and the consideration paid for the stock is different than that in the tender offer, then the transaction violates Rule 14d-10. Rule 14d-10 prohibits a bidder from making a tender offer that is not open to all shareholders or that is made to shareholders at varying prices. Matsushita (D) argues that the Rule is designed to operate only during a specifically defined tender offer period, which in its case expired before the Wasserman transaction. If Rule 14d-10 were rigidly applied only to defined tender offer periods, however, it would be a simple matter for entities to avoid the antidiscrimination goals of the rule. In this case, neither Wasserman nor Matsushita (D) assumed any risk that the tender offer might fail when they crafted their agreement; had the offer failed, they could have backed out. Without the assumption of any additional burden, the offer to Wasserman constituted a special premium over the tender offer.

EDITOR'S ANALYSIS: As with many rules issued by the SEC, the subsequent court construction of Rule 14d-10 has been criticized. The concern is that the interpretation makes the Rule's application too uncertain. Entities engaged in tender offers need to know the full extent of their legal rights with fair certainty, and the ambiguity in the scope of the Rule makes that difficult.

NOTES:

SEC v. CARTER HAWLEY HALE STORES, INC.
760 F.2d 945 (9th Cir. 1985).

NATURE OF CASE: Appeal from denial of preliminary injunction against stock repurchase offer.

FACT SUMMARY: The Limited, Inc. made a tender offer for 55% of Carter Hawley Hale, Inc. (CHH) (D) stock and CHH (D) defeated this via a stock repurchase offer.

CONCISE RULE OF LAW: A stock repurchase offer made in response to a tender offer is not necessarily covered by tender offer rules.

FACTS: The Limited, Inc., making a bid for control of CHH (D), made a tender offer to the shareholders of CHH (D). CHH's (D) management, in response, made a stock repurchase offer to its shareholders as well as an offer of a substantial number of shares in itself to General Cinema Corporation. The market price of the shares steadily crept upward during the repurchase period, which was open-ended in time, to terminate upon the termination of The Limited's tender offer. The repurchase program was terminated when over half the outstanding stock had been repurchased. The SEC (P) then brought suit for injunctive relief, claiming that the repurchase program was in fact a tender offer, and that the disclosure rules of SEC (P) Rule 13e-4 were not met. The district court held the program was not a tender offer.

ISSUE: Is a stock repurchase offer made in response to a tender offer necessarily covered by tender offer rules?

HOLDING AND DECISION: (Skopil, J.) No. A stock repurchase offer made in response to a tender offer is not necessarily covered by tender offer rules. Like the tender offer itself, the nature of the offer must be analyzed in terms of the eight criteria of a tender offer. These are: (1) active and widespread solicitation; (2) solicitation for a substantial percentage of the issuer's stock; (3) a premium price offered; (4) firm as opposed to negotiable terms; (5) the offer being contingent on the tender of a fixed minimum number to be purchased; (6) time limitations; (7) pressure exerted on the offeree; and (8) public announcements of the offer. Here, there was no direct solicitation, no premium price, no negotiable terms, no fixed minimum, no time limitations, and no pressure other than normal market forces. The only criterion squarely met was public announcement. This court does not find this sufficient for the offering to constitute a tender offer, and, therefore, the requirements of 13e-4 did not have to have been met. Affirmed.

EDITOR'S ANALYSIS: The disclosure requirements for tender offers are to be found in SEC Rule 13e-4. This rule prohibits misrepresentation, mandates dissemination of certain facts, and generally tries to guarantee that as much information will be received by shareholders as is possible. Primary enforcement of the rule lies with the SEC.

NOTES:

SCHREIBER v. BURLINGTON NORTHERN, INC.
472 U.S. 1 (1985)

NATURE OF CASE: Appeal from dismissal of action for securities fraud.

FACT SUMMARY: A tender offer in connection with a hostile takeover of a corporation was withdrawn and redone on terms less advantageous to the acquired corporation's shareholders.

CONCISE RULE OF LAW: An element of a cause of action under § 14(e) of the Securities Exchange Act is misrepresentation or nondisclosure.

FACTS: Burlington Northern (D) made a tender offer for a hostile takeover of El Paso Gas Co. Pursuant to this, it offered $24 per share of 25.1 million El Paso shares. Burlington Northern (D) then made a deal with the management of El Paso. The first offer was withdrawn, and then only 21 million shares were purchased. The offerees of the first offer found their tenders to be subject to proration due to the oversubscription of the first offer. Schreiber (P) filed suit, claiming fraud under § 14(e) of the Securities Exchange Act, which prohibited fraudulent practices in connection with a tender offer. There was no allegation that Burlington Northern (D) misrepresented or failed to disclose known material facts. The district court dismissed the suit, and the court of appeals affirmed.

ISSUE: Is an element of a cause of action under § 14(e) of the Securities Exchange Act misrepresentation or nondisclosure?

HOLDING AND DECISION: (Burger, C.J.) Yes. An element of a cause of action under § 14(e) of the Securities Exchange Act is misrepresentation or nondisclosure. Historically, terms such as "fraudulent" or "manipulative," the types of terms used in the section, imply some sort of misrepresentation or nondisclosure. This fits in with the purpose of the Securities Exchange Act, which was to promote full and fair disclosure. Further, the legislative history of the provision and its revisions indicate a concern with misrepresentation, not a desire to create a cause of action for all grievances in connection with a tender offer. Here, since Schreiber (P) did not plead misrepresentation, she has no cause of action. Affirmed.

EDITOR'S ANALYSIS: As the Court stated, the original purpose of the Securities Exchange Act was to promote disclosure. The Court has recognized this in recent years. It has slowly been eroding causes of action under the Act which do not involve misrepresentation.

NOTES:

CTS CORP. v. DYNAMICS CORP. OF AMERICA
481 U.S. 69 (1987).

NATURE OF CASE: Challenge to the constitutionality of Indiana's antitakeover statutes.

FACT SUMMARY: Indiana passed a law that allowed independent shareholders faced with a tender offer to vote as a group to reject the offer and provided that the voting rights of shares were not conferred until fifty days after commencement of the offer.

CONCISE RULE OF LAW: The Williams Act does not preempt state antitakeover legislation that places investors on an equal footing with the takeover bidder.

FACTS: Indiana enacted a control share acquisition statute that denied voting rights of shares to acquiring bidders unless the independent shareholders of the target company voted as a group to grant such rights at a meeting to be held within fifty days of the tender offer. Independent shareholders were considered to be those who were unaffiliated with either the target company or the bidder. The Indiana Act applied to target companies that were incorporated locally, had their principal place of business in Indiana, and had a certain number of shareholders within the state. The Indiana Act was designed to prevent coercive tender offers, where the alternative to tendering the shares is a forced sale at a lower price once the bidder is successful. Bidders asserted that the Williams Act, the federal legislative scheme for corporate takeovers, preempted the Indiana Act. The court of appeals ruled that the Indiana Act was preempted by the Williams Act.

ISSUE: Does the Williams Act preempt state antitakeover legislation that places investors on an equal footing with the takeover bidder?

HOLDING AND DECISION: (Powell, J.) No. The Williams Act does not preempt state antitakeover legislation that places investors on an equal footing with the takeover bidder. In Edgar v. MITE Corp., 457 U.S. 624 (1982), a plurality of the Court ruled that the Williams Act created a careful balance between the interests of offerors and target companies. Thus, state legislation that upset this balance was preempted. Also, the Williams Act states that specific time periods for tender offers may not be altered. In MITE, an Illinois antitakeover statute provided for the potential of an indefinite delay while there was administrative review of the offer. This type of provision is preempted by the Williams Act. The Indiana Act, on the other hand, furthers the basic purpose of the Williams Act by placing investors on an equal footing with the takeover bidder. The Indiana Act does not give either management or the offeror an advantage. Furthermore, the Indiana Act does not impose an absolute fifty-day delay on tender offers. If an offeror fears an adverse shareholder vote, it can make a conditional tender offer, accepting shares on the condition that the shares receive voting rights within a certain period of time. Additionally, the Williams Act does not preempt any delay imposed by the state, only unreasonable delays, such as the indefinite delay in the Illinois law. The delay in the vesting of voting rights for fifty days is not unreasonable because it remains within the sixty-day maximum period that the Williams Act established for tender offers. Therefore, the Indiana Act is not preempted. Reversed.

EDITOR'S ANALYSIS: After this decision, states began to adopt other methods of discouraging hostile takeovers. In 1986, New York enacted a law that prohibited New York companies from making certain business combination transactions for five years after a person acquired more than 20% of the outstanding shares unless there was board consent. The practical effect of the law was to delay the bidder's ownership of the assets of the target company, thus frustrating the bidder's ability to quickly sell off the assets in a "bust-up" transaction.

NOTES:

Notes

CHAPTER 15
THE ENFORCEMENT OF THE SECURITIES LAWS

QUICK REFERENCE RULES OF LAW

1. **The Expanding Panoply of SEC Enforcement Sanctions.** The SEC will issue a cease and desist order, prohibiting further violations, when an individual recklessly issues a tradeability endorsement of a securities offering. (In the Matter of R. William Bradford)

2. **The Criminal Provisions of the Federal Securities Laws.** The willfulness requirement of § 32(a) is satisfied where the defendant is aware that he is doing a wrongful act. (United States v. Dixon)

3. **Mail and Wire Fraud.** Confidential business information is a property right for purposes of the wire and mail fraud statutes. (Carpenter v. United States)

4. **Champion of the Little Guy: The Class Action.** In determining appropriate attorney fees in a class-action litigation, a court should use a "per-centage of the fund" analysis. (Mashburn v. National Healthcare, Inc.)

5. **Recission and Restitution of Contracts in Violation of the Securities Laws.** A court may, upon finding a violation of § 29 of the Securities Exchange Act, award partial rescission. (Regional Properties, Inc. v. Financial & Real Estate Consulting Co.)

6. **Equitable Bars to the Plaintiff's Recovery.** The in pari delicto defense does not preclude defrauded tippees from suing the tipping insider for stock fraud. (Bateman Eichler, Hill Richards, Inc. v. Berner)

7. **Aiding and Abetting.** A financial professional may be liable for aiding and abetting a § 10(b) violation if he has actual knowledge of an independent wrong and substantially assists in the wrong. (Roberts v. Peat, Marwick, Mitchell & Co.)

8. **Aiding and Abetting.** Under federal securities law, a private plaintiff may not maintain a § 10(b) aiding and abetting suit. (Central Bank of Denver v. First Interstate Bank of Denver)

9. **Control Person and Respondeat Superior Liability.** On a theory of "control person" liability, the good faith defense exculpates defendants whose behavior is merely negligent. (Donohoe v. Consolidated Operating & Production Corp.)

10. **The Duties of the Securities Lawyer.** Attorneys who become aware of material inaccuracies in securities documentation presented to their clients abet violations of securities laws if they do not disclose such inaccuracies. (SEC v. National Student Marketing Corp.)

11. **The Duties of the Securities Lawyer.** An attorney, faced with illegal nondisclosure by a client, abets the nondisclosure if he does not act to stop it. (In re Carter and Johnson)

12. **The SEC's Power to Discipline Professionals.** The SEC may pursue enforcement actions against law firms that prepare securities filings. (In re Keating, Muething & Klekamp)

IN THE MATTER OF R. WILLIAM BRADFORD
57 S.E.C. Dock. 1473 (1994).

NATURE OF CASE: Public administrative hearing concerning violations of the Securities Act of 1933.

FACT SUMMARY: Bradford (D) issued a tradeability opinion letter without making any inquiry that would have determined that the shares in question were unregistered.

CONCISE RULE OF LAW: The SEC will issue a cease and desist order, prohibiting further violations, when an individual recklessly issues a tradeability endorsement of a securities offering.

FACTS: Gunderson obtained all shares of Gemaco, Inc. Gunderson fraudulently concealed the fact that he was the sole owner of Gemaco by falsifying stock certificates, shareholder lists, and other documents. Gunderson sent Bradford (D), an attorney, a letter, supposedly from the Gemaco president, which requested a written tradeability opinion. Bradford (D) ignored any evidence that indicated the true nature of the Gemaco shares. Bradford (D) never attempted to contact the supposed president of Gemaco or make any other investigation. Bradford (D) issued the tradeability opinion letter. The SEC instituted an administrative proceeding against Bradford (D).

ISSUE: Will the SEC issue a cease and desist order against an individual who recklessly failed to investigate a securities offering before endorsing its tradeability?

HOLDING AND DECISION: (SEC) Yes. The SEC will issue a cease and desist order, prohibiting further violations, when an individual recklessly issues a tradeability endorsement of a securities offering. In this matter, since the shares would never have been resold without Bradford's (D) opinion letter, Bradford (D) was a cause of the violation of §§ 5(a) and 5(c) of the Securities Act of 1933. Pursuant to § 8A of the Securities Act, Bradford (D) is ordered to cease and desist from committing or causing any further violation of §§ 5(a) and 5(c) of the Securities Act.

EDITOR'S ANALYSIS: This administrative proceeding is a demonstration of the injunctive powers accorded to the SEC in 1990 legislation. The cease and desist order provides the SEC with a trigger mechanism to activate future court proceedings. A violation of the order authorizes a request for civil penalties. Essentially, the cease and desist order lets the SEC give a formal warning without forcing the SEC to initiate an arduous federal court action.

NOTES:

UNITED STATES v. DIXON
536 F.2d 1388 (2d Cir. 1976).

NATURE OF CASE: Appeal from conviction for the failure to disclose loans under § 32(a) of the Exchange Act.

FACT SUMMARY: Dixon (D), president of AVM, attempted to evade SEC (P) disclosure requirements involving a loan from the company.

CONCISE RULE OF LAW: The willfulness requirement of § 32(a) is satisfied where the defendant is aware that he is doing a wrongful act.

FACTS: During most of 1970, Dixon (D), the president of AVM, had an outstanding loan from the company for $65,000. Disclosure requirements mandated that loans to officers above $20,000 be disclosed on the annual report on Form 10-K. Just prior to the close of AVM's fiscal year, Dixon (D) shifted a portion of the loan to his father, had AVM's secretary borrow $5,000 from AVM, and paid off $30,000 with a recently obtained bank loan. As a result, Dixon's (D) debt to AVM was $19,100 at the end of the year, and he did not disclose the loan on the Form 10-K. Shortly thereafter, Dixon (D) took out a new loan from AVM to pay off the bank loan and the secretary's loan from the company. The SEC (P) filed criminal charges against Dixon (D) for willfully violating the reporting requirements. Dixon (D) responded that he believed that year-end indebtedness determined the disclosure mandate. However, the SEC (P) rules require disclosure for loan balances above $20,000 anytime during the year. A jury found Dixon (D) guilty, and he appealed.

ISSUE: Is the willfulness requirement of § 32(a) of the Exchange Act satisfied where the defendant is aware that he is committing a wrongful act?

HOLDING AND DECISION: (Friendly, J.) Yes. The willfulness requirement of § 32(a) of the Exchange Act is satisfied where the defendant is aware that he is doing a wrongful act. A conviction for failure to make proper reports under § 32(a) includes the requirement that the violation be willfully and knowingly committed. A person can willfully violate an SEC (P) rule without knowing of its existence. Thus, this state-of-mind requirement may be established by proof that a defendant realized he was doing a wrongful act. Dixon (D) had loans totaling more than $20,000 during 1970. Therefore, the lack of disclosure was a clear violation. Dixon (D) caused the corporate books of AVM to show debts of the secretary which were in fact his own debts. These acts are wrongful when they lead to the very violations that would have been prevented if the defendant had acted with the aim of scrupulously obeying the rules. Thus, Dixon (D) both violated the rules and had an intent to deceive, which is enough to meet the modest state-of-mind requirement of §32(a). Dixon's (D) conviction is affirmed.

EDITOR'S ANALYSIS: Section 24 of the Securities Act of 1933 contains the criminal provisions for that Act. The only difference between §24 and §32 of the Securities Exchange Act is that §32 adds the "knowingly" requirement. Thus, persons may be prosecuted under §24 as long as the conduct is not accidental. No wrongful intent is required.

NOTES:

CARPENTER v. UNITED STATES
484 U.S. 19 (1987).

NATURE OF CASE: Appeal from conviction for mail and wire fraud.

FACT SUMMARY: Winans (D) and Carpenter (D), employees of the Wall Street Journal, participated in a scheme whereby they traded securities on the basis of advance knowledge of articles that were going to appear in the Journal.

CONCISE RULE OF LAW: Confidential business information is a property right for purposes of the wire and mail fraud statutes.

FACTS: In 1981, Winans (D) was a reporter for the Wall Street Journal and one of the writers of the "Heard on the Street" column. This column was widely read and very influential in the stock market. Carpenter (D) was a news clerk at the Journal. Company policy deemed all information acquired by employees during the course of their employment to be confidential and the property of the Journal. Winans (D) and Carpenter (D) participated in a scheme whereby they relayed advance information on the content of the "Heard" column to brokers, who would trade the subject securities. In 1983 and 1984, Winans (D) and Carpenter (D) made prepublication trades on the basis of advance knowledge of approximately twenty-seven "Heard" columns. The net profit from the scheme was close to $690,000. Winans (D) did not alter journalistic content of the column during the scheme. The SEC (P) discovered the plan and charged Winans (D) and Carpenter (D) with mail and wire fraud. Following their convictions, Winans (D) and Carpenter (D) appealed.

ISSUE: Is confidential business information a property right for purposes of wire and mail fraud statutes?

HOLDING AND DECISION: (White, J.) Yes. Confidential business information is a property right for purposes of wire and mail fraud statutes. 18 U.S.C. §§ 1341 and 1343 prohibit fraudulent schemes that make use of the mail or interstate wire communications. The elements of the offense are a scheme to defraud and the mailing of a letter or placing of a telephone call for the purpose of executing the fraud. In McNally v. United States, 483 U.S. 350 (1987), the Court held that a scheme to defraud does not reach intangible rights. However, the intangible nature of confidential business information does not make it less of a property right for purposes of mail and wire fraud. Confidential business information has long been recognized as property. Wronging someone in his property rights by dishonest methods or schemes qualifies as fraud. The Wall Street Journal's business information that it intended to keep confidential was its property. Winans (D) and Carpenter (D) were aware of this policy and appropriated the information for their own use. Therefore, Winans (D) and Carpenter (D) schemed to defraud the Journal of its property and violated federal mail and wire fraud statutes. Affirmed.

EDITOR'S ANALYSIS: Some commentators have questioned this decision because it seems to effectively overrule the decision in McNally. They point out that whenever an employee acts in a way contrary to the interest of the employer there could be some violation of intangible property rights. see Coffee, Hush! the Criminal Status of Confidential Information After McNally and Carpenter and the Enduring Problem of Overcriminalization, 26 Am. Crim. L. Rev. 121 (1988).

NOTES:

MASHBURN v. NATIONAL HEALTHCARE, INC.
684 F. Supp. 679 (M.D. Ala. 1988).

NATURE OF CASE: Determination of attorney fees in a class action settlement.

FACT SUMMARY: After approving a settlement of a class-action securities litigation, the court was called upon to determine appropriate attorney fees.

CONCISE RULE OF LAW: In determining appropriate attorney fees in a class-action litigation, a court should use a "per-centage of the fund" analysis.

FACTS: As a result of a stock offering in National Healthcare, Inc. (D), which eventually went bad, a class-action suit on behalf of the shareholders (P) was brought against National Healthcare (D), its principals (D), and various financial professionals (D). The matter was eventually settled for $17,425,000, including over $9 million in cash. The court was then called upon to determine appropriate attorney fees.

ISSUE: In determining appropriate attorney fees in a class action litigation, should a court use a "percentage of the fund" analysis?

HOLDING AND DECISION: Yes. In determining appropriate attorney fees in a class-action litigation, a court should use a "percentage of the fund" analysis. An exception to the usual rule that all parties bear their own legal fees is the "common fund" rule, which provides that when the work of a few attorneys creates a fund for the benefit of others those attorneys are entitled to a share in the funds, i.e., the gross recovery. A traditional alternative to the percentage of the fund approach is the so-called "lodestar" approach. This method involves a multiplication of hours spent and the prevailing hourly rate, with the lodestar amount adjusted upwards or downwards depending on such factors as expertise, contingency, difficulty of the issues involved, and so on. While this approach may be best for statutory fee awards, the best approach in a common fund situation is simply to take a percentage of the fund, i.e., 20 to 30%, and adjust it downwards or upwards on the basis of the same factors analyzed in the lodestar approach. This approach is better because it rewards economy. The lodestar approach looks at time spent, which encourages time padding; the percentage approach only looks to results. Unlike the lodestar system, it encourages early settlement and discourages protracted litigation. [The court then made its determination of appropriate fees using, as a cautionary measure, both approaches. The court held that hours spent at the customary billing rate equalled $1 million, to which it added a multiplier of 3.122 as a result of contingency, results obtained, and delay in receipt of fees. The court noted that this award of $3,272,206.60 was roughly equivalent to 19.5% of the case settlement, just below the 20 to 30% "benchmark" percentage fee award, and therefore a clearly reasonable amount.]

EDITOR'S ANALYSIS: Despite the opinion here, the lodestar approach remains the most common method of calculating fees in a class action. The two seminal cases involving the lodestar analysis were Lindy Brothers, Inc. of Philadelphia v. American Radiator, 487 F.2d 161 (3rd Cir. 1973), and Johnson v. Georgia Highway Express, 488 F.2d 714 (5th Cir. 1974). The Johnson court adopted twelve factors to aid in determining a fee award, including the novelty of the questions involved in the case, the case's "undesirability," and the experience and reputation of the attorneys.

NOTES:

REGIONAL PROPERTIES, INC. v. FINANCIAL & REAL ESTATE CONSULTING CO.
678 F.2d 552 (5th Cir. 1982).

NATURE OF CASE: Appeal from order partly rescinding partnership agreements for violation of § 29(b) of the Securities Exchange Act.

FACT SUMMARY: A district court, having found a violation of § 29(b) of the Securities Exchange Act, partly rescinded the transactions.

CONCISE RULE OF LAW: A court may, upon finding a violation of § 29 of the Securities Exchange Act, award partial rescission.

FACTS: Thomas (P) and Shipley (P) entered into an arrangement with Financial and Real Estate Consultants Co. (D) and its principal, Goldner (D), to act as general partner in a series of real estate development limited partnerships promoted by Financial (D). It later turned out that neither Goldner (D) nor Financial (D) had registered as broker-dealers with the SEC as required by securities laws. Thomas (P) and Shipley (P) and their company, Regional (P), filed an action against Financial (D) seeking rescission of the various agreements, return of all monies paid, and the right to retain all monies in escrow. The district court held the partnership agreements voidable. However, rather than canceling all transactions, the court allowed the partnerships already in operation to continue and ordered return of the funds in escrow. Both sides appealed.

ISSUE: May a court, upon finding a violation of § 29 of the Securities Exchange Act, partly rescind the transaction?

HOLDING AND DECISION: (Rubin, J.) Yes. A court, upon finding a violation of § 29 of the Securities Exchange Act, may award partial rescission. Section 29 provides that every contract made in violation of the Act shall be void as to the violating party. Here, Financial (D) and Goldner (D) acted as broker-dealers without registering with the SEC in violation of the Act. Whether Regional (P) can rescind the agreements requires an analysis of § 29. The first issue is whether the section implies a private right of action. None is expressly created. However, absent such a right, its usefulness is open to serious question. Consequently, inferring such a right appears consonant with congressional intent in the securities laws. The next question is what the elements of a cause of action might be. The language of the section implies three: (1) the construct involved a prohibited transaction, (2) privity, and (3) status of a plaintiff as an intended protected person under the law. All three of these elements are present here. This leads to the final issue, the remedy. The district court, having found the contracts voidable, refused to return the parties to the status quo ante because circumstances had changed to the point that such return was impossible. It therefore voided the agreements only prospectively. Both sides contend that the court could not do this. This is incorrect. Rescission is, even if statutorily authorized, an equitable remedy. Courts are free to fashion equitable remedies as they see fit. Consequently, the district court acted within its rights in fashioning the remedy it did. Remanded for a consideration of Financial's (D) possible equitable defenses.

EDITOR'S ANALYSIS: On remand, the appeals court barred Financial's (D) use of equitable defenses on the grounds that it had unclean hands. The court found that Financial (D) had deliberately misrepresented the amount of experience it had, its registration status, and the fact that one of its lawyers had been disbarred. Absent unclean hands, all the traditional equitable defenses — e.g., laches, estoppel, waiver, etc. — would typically be available to a § 29(b) defendant.

NOTES:

BATEMAN EICHLER, HILL RICHARDS, INC. v. BERNER
472 U.S. 299 (1985).

NATURE OF CASE: Review of judgment awarding damages for Rule 10b-5 violations.

FACT SUMMARY: After Berner (P) traded on false insider tips supplied by brokers at Bateman Eichler (D), Bateman Eichler (D) contended that Berner's (P) own culpability barred his private action for damages.

CONCISE RULE OF LAW: The in pari delicto defense does not preclude defrauded tippees from suing the tipping insider for stock fraud.

FACTS: Lazzaro (D) was an employee of brokerage firm Bateman Eichler, Hill Richards, Inc. (D). Falsely contending that he had inside information regarding growth prospects for a certain corporation, he induced Berner (P) and numerous other investors (P) to purchase stock in the corporation. The investors (P) later sued for violations of Rule 10b-5. Bateman Eichler (D) contended that, since the investors (P) had themselves attempted to trade on inside, albeit incorrect, information, they were barred from recovery under the in pari delicto defense. This contention was rejected by the district court and the court of appeals. The Supreme Court granted review.

ISSUE: Does the in pari delicto defense preclude defrauded tippees from suing the tipping insider for stock fraud?

HOLDING AND DECISION: (Brennan, J.) No. The in pari delicto defense does not preclude defrauded tippees from suing the tipping insider for stock fraud. Traditionally, the in pari delicto defense precluded recovery by a wrongdoing plaintiff on the notion that courts should not lend aid to wrongdoers. The doctrine's vitality continues to the present. However, the doctrine will not bar a suit where (1) the defendant's wrongdoing equals or outweighs the plaintiff's and (2) allowing the suit will serve important public purposes. In the context of an insider trading situation, the wrong by the securities professional (supplying the insider information) exceeds that of the investors, as the professional is under ethical obligations not imposed on the general public. Further, this Court believes that the public interest is served by allowing suits of this nature, so as to discourage tipping by insiders. Consequently, the suit here is not barred by in pari delicto. Affirmed.

EDITOR'S ANALYSIS: The rules of tippers and tippees in the arena of securities laws are quite different. Generally speaking, a tippee does not violate securities laws by trading on inside information, per Chiarella v. United States, 445 U.S. 222 (1980). The tipper, if he trades on his own information, commits a 10b-5 violation.

ROBERTS v. PEAT, MARWICK, MITCHELL & CO.
857 F.2d 646 (9th Cir. 1989), cert. denied, 493 U.S. 1002.

NATURE OF CASE: Appeal from dismissal of securities fraud violation.

FACT SUMMARY: Investors contended that accounting firm Peat, Marwick (D) was liable as an abettor to a Rule 10b-5 violation.

CONCISE RULE OF LAW: A financial professional may be liable for aiding and abetting a § 10(b) violation if he has actual knowledge of an independent wrong and substantially assists in the wrong.

FACTS: During the early 1980s, a number of limited partnerships relating to petroleum reclamation were sold with Heim (D) acting as general partner. The accounting firm of Peat, Marwick, Mitchell & Co. (D) acted as accountant and auditor. The ventures turned out to be unprofitable, and numerous investors (P), including Roberts (P), brought suit alleging violations of § 10(b) of the Exchange Act and Rule 10b-5. The investors (P) alleged that Peat, Marwick (D) aided and abetted the fraudulent scheme. The district court granted Peat, Marwick's (D) motion to dismiss for failure to state a claim, and the investors (P) appealed.

ISSUE: May a financial professional be liable for aiding and abetting a § 10(b) violation if he knows of and assists in an independent wrong?

HOLDING AND DECISION: (Per curiam) Yes. A financial professional may be liable for aiding and abetting a § 10(b) violation if he knows of and assists in an independent wrong. Aiding and abetting a fraudulent securities transaction is itself a violation of Rule 10b-5. The three elements of an aiding and abetting 10b-5 cause of action are: (1) the existence of an independent wrong; (2) actual knowledge by the aider of that wrong, and (3) substantial assistance in the perpetration of that wrong. Further, if an alleged aider had a duty to disclose, silence in the face of a known misstatement by the principal may satisfy the third criterion. Here, as an independent auditor, Peat, Marwick (D) had a duty to disclose to investors (P), and if it can be proven that it intentionally hid unfavorable facts, it may be liable as an abettor. [The court also affirmed a dismissal as to the law firm Houston Harbaugh (D), concluding that it had had no duty running to the investors (P).] Reversed in part; affirmed in part.

EDITOR'S ANALYSIS: Suits against financial professionals in securities cases are common. The usual scenario is that the truly guilty party, the promoter of the soured deal, is bankrupt or gone. This often leaves the lawyer or accountant as the only source of funds and, therefore, the target of the inevitable suit.

CENTRAL BANK OF DENVER, N.A. v. FIRST INTERSTATE BANK OF DENVER, N.A.
114 S. Ct. 1439 (1994).

NATURE OF CASE: Appeal from the reversal of a grant of defendant's motion for summary judgment in an action for aiding and abetting securities fraud.

FACT SUMMARY: After Central Bank (D) postponed an appraisal of land related to a construction project involving two bond issues, First Interstate (P), a bond purchaser, sued when the issuer defaulted on the bonds, alleging Central Bank (D) was secondarily liable for aiding and abetting a fraud.

CONCISE RULE OF LAW: Under federal securities law, a private plaintiff may not maintain a § 10(b) aiding and abetting suit.

FACTS: Central Bank (D) served as indenture trustee for two bond issues made by the Colorado Building Authority (D). The bond covenants required that the land be worth at least 160% of the bonds' outstanding principal and interest. When the underwriter expressed concern that the 160% test was not being met, Central Bank's (D) in-house appraiser suggested retaining an outside appraiser. At the request of AmWest (D), provider of the last appraisal, Central Bank (D) agreed to delay the independent review. Before independent review was completed, the Authority (D) defaulted on the bonds. First Interstate (P), purchaser of a large portion of the second bond issue, filed suit, alleging primary violations of § 10(b) of the Securities Exchange Act of 1934 and alleging that Central Bank (D) was secondarily liable for aiding and abetting the fraud. The district court granted summary judgment to Central Bank (D). The court of appeals reversed. Central Bank (D) appealed.

ISSUE: Under federal securities law, may a private plaintiff maintain a § 10(b) aiding and abetting suit?

HOLDING AND DECISION: (Kennedy, J.) No. Under federal securities law, a private plaintiff may not maintain a § 10(b) aiding and abetting suit. If Congress intended to impose aiding and abetting liability, it would have used those words in the statutory text. A plaintiff must show reliance on the defendant's misstatement or omission to recover under Rule 10b-5. If the aiding and abetting action proposed in this case were allowed, Central Bank (D) could be liable without any showing that First Interstate (P) relied upon Central Bank's (D) statements or actions. The absence of § 10(b) aiding and abetting liability does not mean that secondary actors in the securities markets are always free from liability. They may be liable as primary violators under Rule 10b-5, assuming all of the requirements for such liability are met. First Interstate (P) concedes, however, that Central Bank (D) did not commit a manipulative or deceptive act within the meaning of § 10(b). The judgment of the court of appeals is reversed.

DISSENT: (Stevens, J.) All eleven courts of appeals have recognized a private cause of action against aiders and abettors under § 10(b) and Rule 10b-5. A settled construction of an important federal statute should not be disturbed unless and until Congress so decides. The available evidence suggests congressional approval of aider and abettor liability in private § 10(b) actions. The principle the majority espouses is inconsistent with long-established Commission and judicial precedent.

EDITOR'S ANALYSIS: The Securities Act of 1933 regulates initial distributions of securities, while the Securities Exchange Act of 1934, for the most part, regulates postdistribution trading. Together, the Acts embrace a fundamental purpose to substitute a philosophy of full disclosure for the philosophy of caveat emptor. The Acts create an extensive scheme of civil liability, including express and implied private rights of action.

NOTES:

DONOHOE v. CONSOLIDATED OPERATING & PRODUCTION CORP.

30 F.3d 907 (7th Cir. 1994).

NATURE OF CASE: Appeal of summary judgment in favor of defendants in action alleging securities violations.

FACT SUMMARY: Fifty-four investors, including Donohoe (P), were lured into investing in an ill-fated oil drilling project by an individual they claimed was controlled by shareholders Nortman (D) and Berrettini (D).

CONCISE RULE OF LAW: On a theory of "control person" liability, the good faith defense exculpates defendants whose behavior is merely negligent.

FACTS: Donohoe (P) and fifty-three other investors (P) were lured into investing in COPCO (D) by Bridges (D), a principal and shareholder. The project involved drilling for oil on land that was known by Bridges (D) to lack oil. Bridges (D) clearly defrauded everyone, but a question remained as to whether Nortman (D) and Berrettini (D), two other principals and shareholders who lost $100,000 of their own money, knew of the fraud. They had performed a background check on Bridges (D), but they were forced to rely on his expertise in the field. Donohoe (P) and other investors (P) sued, contending that Norman (D) and Berrettini (D) had controlled Bridges (D) and were therefore liable for his malfeasance under a "control person" theory. The district court granted summary judgment to Nortman (D) and Berrettini (D) without addressing Donohoe's (P) "control person" theory, so the appellate court remanded for consideration of that theory. On remand, the district court concluded that Nortman (D) and Berrettini (D) had met the good faith defense for control persons under the securities laws. The investors (P) appealed again.

ISSUE: On a theory of "control person" liability, does the good faith defense exculpate defendants whose behavior is merely negligent?

HOLDING AND DECISION: (Cudahy, J.) Yes. On a theory of "control person" liability, the good faith defense exculpates defendants whose behavior is merely negligent. Control person liability is most generally used in a respondeat superior context to hold a brokerage house liable for the securities violations committed by its employees. Outside of that setting, a more flexible approach is used; the question to be answered is whether the control person took reasonable measures, in the particular situation, to prevent the securities violation. In this case, Nortman (D) and Berrettini (D) took steps to prevent fraud. Whether their steps were perfect is not at issue; they did enough to merit a good faith defense to control person liability. Affirmed.

EDITOR'S ANALYSIS: The circuits are split as to the purpose of the control person provisions contained in the Securities Act and in the Exchange Act. Some circuits treat the provisions as a requirement that controlling persons must attempt to prevent harms. Other circuits read the provisions as requiring some form of culpability on the part of the controlling person. The entire area of control person liability remains unsettled in the law.

NOTES:

SEC v. NATIONAL STUDENT MARKETING CORP.
457 F. Supp. 682 (D.D.C. 1978).

NATURE OF CASE: Appeal from injunctions issued in securities fraud action.

FACT SUMMARY: While representing a merger target, Lord, Bissell and Brooks (D) declined to disclose potentially unfavorable information about the suitor corporation to the target's shareholders.

CONCISE RULE OF LAW: Attorneys who become aware of material inaccuracies in securities documentation presented to their clients abet violations of securities laws if they do not disclose such inaccuracies.

FACTS: National Student Marketing Corp. (NSMC) (D) sought to acquire Interstate National Corporation. Interstate's board acquiesced, with certain provisions. One condition was receipt of a comfort letter from NSMC's (D) auditors regarding the soundness of NSMC's (D) finances for the months since its last annual audit. At the meeting of the two corporations' boards at which the merger was to be consummated, such a letter, albeit unsigned and not in conformity with the merger agreement, was presented to Interstate's attorney, Lord, Bissel & Brook (D), which in turn gave it to Interstate's board. With this, the merger was effected. Several days later, however, an amended letter was sent that documented certain weaknesses in NSMC's (D) finances. Lord, Bissel & Brook's (D) attorneys never disclosed this to the former Interstate shareholders, who had received NSMC (D) stock in exchange for their shares. Later, acting on shareholder complaints, the SEC (P) held Lord, Bissel & Brooks (D) liable as an abettor to a securities law violation, in that misleading assertions had been made regarding the NSMC (D) stock in violation of Rule 10b-5. The SEC (P) issued an injunction against Lord, Bissell & Brooks (D) prohibiting further violations. Lord, Bissell & Brooks (D) appealed.

ISSUE: Do attorneys who become aware of material inaccuracies in securities documentation presented to their clients abet violations of securities laws if they do not disclose such inaccuracies?

HOLDING AND DECISION: (Parker, J.) Yes. Attorneys who become aware of material inaccuracies in securities documentation presented to their clients abet securities laws violations if they do not disclose such inaccuracies. A party abets a securities law violation if three elements are satisfied: (1) a violation by a principal; (2) knowledge of the violation; and (3) an assistance in the violation. The first two elements are usually clear-cut; the problem is deciding what exactly constitutes "assistance." Here, it is undisputed that a securities law violation occurred, as the comfort letter relied upon by Interstate's board was materially inaccurate. Lord, Bissell & Brooks (D) became aware of the inaccuracies when it received the corrected letter. The issue thus becomes whether Lord, Bissel and Brooks (D) assisted the securities law violation. This requires a resolution of the issue as to whether inaction can constitute assistance. This court is of the opinion that inaction in conjunction with a duty to disclose constitutes assistance. Here, Interstate's attorneys, Lord, Bissel, & Brooks (D), had a fiduciary duty, which includes disclosure of information relevant to its finances. Thus, having failed to disclose, Lord, Bissel & Brooks (D) abetted the law violation. [The court went on to hold, however, that there was insufficient evidence of potential future violations by Lord, Bissel & Brooks (D), so injunctive relief was unwarranted.] Reversed.

EDITOR'S ANALYSIS: Much of the analysis in this case, and in many other cases dealing with aiding and abetting, was made moot by the case Central Bank of Denver v. First Interstate Bank of Denver, 511 U.S.164 (1994) 62 U.S.L.W. 4230 (1994). In that case, the Supreme Court abolished aider and abettor liability for actions under § 10(b) of the 1934 Act and Rule 10b-5. Since most private enforcement actions are based on § 10(b), this represents a drastic change in the legal landscape.

NOTES:

IN RE CARTER AND JOHNSON

Sec. Ex. Comm., Fed. Sec. L. Rep. (CCH), ¶ 82, 847 (1981).

NATURE OF CASE: Appeal from order censuring attorneys.

FACT SUMMARY: The SEC (P) accused Carter (D) and Johnson (D), attorneys for National Telephone Co., of aiding and abetting illegal nondisclosure by a National Telephone officer.

CONCISE RULE OF LAW: An attorney, faced with illegal nondisclosure by a client, abets the nondisclosure if he does not act to stop it.

FACTS: Carter (D) and Johnson (D) were partners at the law firm representing National Telephone Co. They were involved in the drafting of a contingent financing plan, called the "lease maintenance plan" (LMP), which, if triggered, would result in the company's dissolution. Hart, National's CEO, refused to release a Form 8-K disclosing the existence of the LMP. During the next year, Carter (D) and Johnson (D) urged Hart to disclose the terms of the LMP, but he did not. Eventually, the LMP was triggered. At this point Hart even asked the attorneys to draft an opinion stating that disclosure of the LMP was not necessary, in flagrant opposition to their advice. Johnson (D) and Carter (D) refused. Hart later resigned. The SEC (P) brought an action against Carter (D) and Johnson (D) contending that they aided and abetted Hart's illegal nondisclosure. An Administrative Law Judge agreed, and Carter (D) and Johnson (D) appealed.

ISSUE: Does an attorney, faced with illegal nondisclosure by a client, abet the nondisclosure if he does not act to stop it?

HOLDING AND DECISION: Yes. An attorney, faced with illegal nondisclosure by a client, abets the nondisclosure if he does not act to stop it. However, for such aiding and abetting to occur there must be intent on the part of the attorney to intend to aid the violation through inaction or inaction in conscious disregard to an attorney's ethical obligations with respect to disclosure. Here, the frequent urging of Hart by Carter (D) and Johnson (D) to disclose the particulars of the LMP demonstrate a lack of intent to aid and abet. As to the attorney's obligations to effect disclosure, these obligations have never been sufficiently formulated to impose a standard apart from general obligations not to assist in commission of a crime. Based on the record, no such general obligation was breached by Carter (D) or Johnson (D). Reversed. Although not applicable to this case, the SEC (P) is now on notice that attorneys have certain obligations with respect to disclosure. In essence, when a lawyer with significant responsibilities in the effectuation of a company's compliance with the disclosure requirements of the federal securities laws becomes aware that his client is engaged in a substantial and continuing failure to satisfy those disclosure requirements, his continued participation violates professional standards unless he takes prompt steps to show that he has not been co-opted into the scheme of nondisclosure.

EDITOR'S ANALYSIS: The last standard promulgated by the SEC leaves much to be desired in terms of clarity. It is not stated how significant "significant" has to be. Also, exactly how drastic the steps to end the noncompliance must be is an issue that will no doubt spawn much future litigation.

NOTES:

IN RE KEATING, MUETHING & KLEKAMP, EXCHANGE ACT RELEASE NO. 15,982
Fed. Sec. L. Rep. 82,124 (July 2, 1979)

NATURE OF CASE: Administrative hearing to determine alleged violations of SEC disclosure requirements.

FACT SUMMARY: The SEC (P) brought an enforcement action against Keating, Muething & Klekamp (KMK) (D), a law firm, for alleged violations of reporting requirements as primary counsel for American Financial Corporation (AFC).

CONCISE RULE OF LAW: The SEC may pursue enforcement actions against law firms that prepare securities filings.

FACTS: From the early 1960s until 1976, KMK (D) was the primary law firm for AFC. KMK (D) provided legal services for AFC and its subsidiaries for nearly all aspects of the business. Keating was a founding member of KMK (D) until 1972, when he became Executive Vice President of AFC. Keating also owned a large share of the outstanding stock of AFC. Other partners in KMK (D) served on the board of directors of AFC's subsidiaries. Beginning in 1972, AFC and its subsidiaries repeatedly failed to make full disclosure in SEC (P) filings regarding six self-dealing transactions. These transactions included a purchase by Klekamp of AFC common stock with funds advanced by an AFC subsidiary. Klekamp could not repay the loan, and the subsidiary agreed not to hold Klekamp personally liable. A filing with the SEC (P) reported that nearly the entire amount of the loan was collected, when in fact the subsidiary had agreed to write off the majority of the original loan. The KMK (D) partner who filed the SEC (P) documents relied totally on the representations of Klekamp and conducted no investigation of the true nature of the transaction. The SEC (P) then sought an enforcement action against KMK (D) for violations of the reporting requirements.

ISSUE: May the SEC pursue enforcement actions against law firms that prepare securities filings?

HOLDING AND DECISION: Yes. The SEC (P) may pursue enforcement actions against law firms that prepare securities filings. Law firms have the duty to make sure that disclosure documents filed with the SEC (P) include all material facts about a client of which it has knowledge as a result of its legal representation. While the SEC (P) may not mandate specific internal procedures for meeting this duty, some system to insure professional standards is required. The SEC (P) may pursue enforcement actions against an entire law firm where the firm collectively had knowledge of material transactions that are not properly reported. Virtually every member of KMK (D) was aware of the transactions that were incorrectly reported to the SEC (P). Therefore, an enforcement action against KMK (D) is reasonable under these circumstances. KMK (D) offered a settlement whereby they agree to adopt and maintain internal and supervisory procedures designed to ensure that the disclosure requirements of federal securities laws are complied with. The SEC (P) may accept this settlement.

DISSENT: (Karmel, C.) It is repugnant to our adversary system of legal representation to permit the SEC (P) to discipline attorneys who act as counsel to regulated persons. While Congress had provided for express authority to regulate accountants, there is no substantive authority for the SEC (P) to prosecute attorneys by way of an administrative remedy.

EDITOR'S ANALYSIS: Commissioner Karmel later published a book detailing her position against the SEC's (P) use of attorneys to carry out the disclosure requirements. She takes issue with the position that the SEC (P) is a small, understaffed agency which must depend on the issuer's counsel. Karmel insists that an adversarial relationship between the attorneys and the SEC (P) exists.

NOTES:

CHAPTER 16
REGULATION OF THE SECURITIES MARKET AND SECURITIES PROFESSIONALS

QUICK REFERENCE RULES OF LAW

1. **Self-Regulation.** Failure to repay a loan from a client does not in itself constitute unethical behavior by a securities broker. (In re Robert Jautz)

2. **Direct SEC Supervision of Brokers and Dealers.** Persons occupying positions in the legal or compliance departments of broker-dealers may be considered supervisors where they have a requisite degree of responsibility, ability, or authority to affect the conduct of the employee whose behavior is at issue. (In the Matter of John Gutfreund et al.)

3. **"Know Your Security.** A securities dealer may be barred from participation in the securities market if he makes uninformed predictions about an investment. (Hanly v. SEC)

4. **Suitability.** So long as offering materials made available to limited partners accurately reflect the suitability of the investment for the individual investors, such investors may not reasonably rely on contrary oral assurances by their brokers. (Brown v. E.F. Hutton Group, Inc.)

5. **Churning and Other "Relational" Frauds.** Excessive trading, or "churning," occurs when a broker buys and sells securities for a customer's account without regard to the customer's investment interests, for the purpose of generating commissions. (Merrill Lynch, Pierce, Fenner & Smith v. Arceneaux)

6. **Arbitration.** If a fraud claim relates to a contract as a whole, and the contract contains an arbitration clause, the Federal Arbitration Act requires the fraud claim to be decided by an arbitrator. (R.M. Perez & Associates, Inc. v. Welch)

7. **Broker-Dealer and Inside Information.** In the context of insider trading, a person whose liability is solely derivative is not as culpable as one whose breach of duty gave rise to the liability in the first place. (Bateman Eichler, Hill Richards, Inc. v. Berner)

IN RE ROBERT JAUTZ
Sec. Ex. Comm., Ex. Act Rel. #24346 (1987).

NATURE OF CASE: Appeal from NASD disciplinary action for exploitation of position.

FACT SUMMARY: The NASD concluded that Jautz (D) had violated its ethical rules by soliciting a loan from a client and by not repaying the loan.

CONCISE RULE OF LAW: Failure to repay a loan from a client does not in itself constitute unethical behavior by a securities broker.

FACTS: For over ten years, Jautz (D) had acted as stockbroker for "M" and her late husband. In 1984, in bad financial straits, Jautz (D) approached "M" about a loan. "M" agreed to loan Jautz (D) $2,000, repayable in three months at 15% interest. Jautz (D) was unable to repay the loan. "M" complained to the National Association of Securities Dealers (NASD), which found Jautz (D) in violation of its Rules of Fair Practice. He was fined $500 and censured. He appealed to the SEC.

ISSUE: Does failure to repay a loan from a client in itself constitute unethical behavior by a securities broker?

HOLDING AND DECISION: No. A failure to repay a loan from a client does not in itself constitute unethical behavior by a securities broker. A breach of contract violates NASD standards only if it is committed in bad faith or accompanied by unethical conduct. Failure to repay a loan is, in essence, a breach of contract. Here, however, there was no allegation that Jautz (D) used any sort of coercion, misrepresentation, or other devious means to secure the loan or that he failed to repay it for any reason other than lack of funds. This was, although not exemplary behavior, not unethical behavior. Reversed.

EDITOR'S ANALYSIS: There is a certain amount of self-regulation in the securities industry. As can be seen here, the NASD polices its members. Also regulating themselves are the various stock exchanges. Above these authorities is the SEC, providing governmental regulation.

NOTES:

IN THE MATTER OF JOHN GUTFREUND ET AL.
Fed. Sec. L. Rep. (CCH) ¶85,067 (Admin. Proc., Dec. 3, 1992).

NATURE OF CASE: Action by the SEC against senior officials of an investment banking firm for failing to properly supervise employees.

FACT SUMMARY: In this SEC action involving serious misconduct by a senior official at Salomon Brothers (D) — misconduct that had been brought to the attention of the firm's chief legal officer — the SEC (P) discussed the responsibilities of legal and compliance officers found to be "supervisors" in such firms.

CONCISE RULE OF LAW: Persons occupying positions in the legal or compliance departments of broker-dealers may be considered supervisors where they have a requisite degree of responsibility, ability, or authority to affect the conduct of the employee whose behavior is at issue.

FACTS: After it was discovered that the head of the Government Trading desk at Salomon Brothers, Inc. (D) had submitted a large false bid to the United States Treasury, action was taken by the SEC (P) against senior officials of Salomon Brothers (D) for failure to properly supervise that employee. Feuerstein, Saloman's (D) chief legal officer, found out about the false bids in 1991 when the other officers were informed. He advised the officers that it was a criminal act and should be reported to the SEC (P). However, he did not follow up when the report was not forthcoming, and he did not recommend any procedures to deter future misconduct. Because Feuerstein was not a direct supervisor of the employee who submitted the false bid, the SEC (P) did not take action against him personally. However, it did issue a report concerning the compliance responsibilities of persons who occupy positions of authority in brokerage firms.

ISSUE: May persons occupying positions in the legal or compliance departments of broker-dealers be considered supervisors where they have the requisite degree of responsibility, ability, or authority to affect the conduct of the employee whose behavior is at issue?

HOLDING AND DECISION: Yes. Persons occupying positions in the legal or compliance departments of broker-dealers may be considered supervisors where they have the requisite degree of responsibility, ability, or authority to affect the conduct of the employee whose behavior is at issue. Once a person in Feuerstein's position becomes involved in formulating management's response to the problem, he or she is obligated to take affirmative steps to ensure that appropriate action is taken to address the misconduct. If such a person takes appropriate steps but management fails to act, he or she should consider what additional steps are appropriate to address the matter. Once such a person is deemed to have supervisory obligations, he must either discharge those responsibilities or know that others are taking appropriate action.

EDITOR'S ANALYSIS: The additional steps to be taken by supervisors may include disclosure of the matter to the entity's board of directors, resignation from the firm, or disclosure to regulatory authorities. In the case of an attorney, however, the applicable Code of Professional Responsibility and the Canons of Ethics may bear upon what course of conduct that individual may properly pursue.

NOTES:

HANLY v. SEC
415 F.2d 589 (2d. Cir. 1969).

NATURE OF CASE: Appeal from order barring certain individuals from acting as securities salesmen.

FACT SUMMARY: Hanly (P) and four other securities dealers (P) were suspended from participation in the securities field by the SEC (D) for having made extremely overly optimistic predictions about an investment based on issuer information.

CONCISE RULE OF LAW: A securities dealer may be barred from participation in the securities market if he makes uninformed predictions about an investment.

FACTS: U.S. Sonics Corporation was engaged in the electronics business. Its finances had been marginal at best. It developed a certain filter which had the potential to be a big seller, but the prospects never materialized. Eventually the corporation went bankrupt. During this time, Hanly (P) and four other securities salesmen (P), mostly using information provided by U.S. Sonics, made glowing recommendations to potential investors, many of whom purchased stock in the corporation. When their investments became worthless, complaints were made. The SEC (D), finding the salespeople's (P) conduct to have been egregious, suspended them from the industry. They appealed.

ISSUE: May a securities dealer be barred from participation in the securities market if he makes uninformed predictions about an investment?

HOLDING AND DECISION: (Timbers, J.) Yes. a securities dealer may be barred from participation in the securities market if he makes uninformed predictions about a market. Brokers and salesmen are under a duty to be knowledgeable about the securities they sell. This necessarily involves a duty to investigate claims made by an issuer. They cannot blindly accept recommendations and assertions made in sales literature. This duty arises out of the special relationship between the broker and the purchaser. Here, the salespeople (P) made recommendations without any knowledge sufficient upon which to base such recommendation, and this was a clear violation of duty. Affirmed.

EDITOR'S ANALYSIS: A Rule 10b-5 violation requires scienter. It would seem clear that an inaccurate recommendation does not rise to the level of scienter. In most cases, a reckless failure to research prior to recommendation would be the sort of situation where a 10b-5 violation would occur.

NOTES:

BROWN v. E.F. HUTTON GROUP INC.
991 F.2d 1020 (2d Cir. 1993).

NATURE OF CASE: Appeal of summary judgment dismissing claim of § 10(b) unsuitability.

FACT SUMMARY: Four hundred investors (P) lost money as limited partners in a fund that acquired properties upon which existing oil and gas wells were located.

CONCISE RULE OF LAW: So long as offering materials made available to limited partners accurately reflect the suitability of the investment for the individual investors, such investors may not reasonably rely on contrary oral assurances by their brokers.

FACTS: Brown (P) was one of 400 investors (P) in a limited partnership organized to acquire properties upon which existing oil and gas wells were located. The investors (P) were generally unsophisticated in relation to the world of petroleum investment. Hutton (D) issued a brochure that described the investment in generally positive terms and a prospectus which clearly disclosed numerous risks involved in the investment. Hutton (D) account executives painted a rosy picture of the investment when making their sales pitches, representing it as a low-risk, conservative venture. Once the investment became worthless, Brown (P) and other investors (P) filed suit, contending that they had been misled by Hutton's (D) account executives into purchasing unsuitable securities. The court granted summary judgment for Hutton (D), and Brown (P) appealed.

ISSUE: May investors reasonably rely on contrary oral assertions by their brokers when offering materials accurately reflect investment suitability?

HOLDING AND DECISION: (Jacobs, J.) No. So long as offering materials made available to limited partners accurately reflect the suitability of the investment for the individual investors, such investors may not reasonably rely on contrary oral assurances by their brokers. To prevail in a § 10(b) unsuitability claim, a plaintiff must prove that the securities he purchased were unsuited to his needs and that the defendant knew it and recommended the purchase anyway, making misrepresentations upon which the plaintiff relied to his detriment. In this case, each investor (P) received written materials detailing the risky nature of the investment. While the investors (P) were generally not a sophisticated group, reliance upon oral representations alone is not justified as a matter of law when detailed written information contradicts the oral assurances. It was the duty of the investors (P) to determine suitability when they had sufficiently detailed information. Affirmed.

EDITOR'S ANALYSIS: Courts have been much less forgiving of investors that fail to read detailed investment information than has the SEC. Courts generally take the position that investors cannot be misled if relevant information is disclosed in a publication. However, this ignores the fact that most investors seek out a broker because they lack the expertise to make investment decisions for themselves.

NOTES:

MERRILL LYNCH, PIERCE, FENNER & SMITH v. ARCENEAUX
767 F.2d 1498 (11th Cir. 1985).

NATURE OF CASE: Appeal from judgment awarding damages for securities laws violations.

FACT SUMMARY: After sustaining a $45,697 net loss in fifteen months, Arceneaux (P) contended that broker Merrill Lynch (D) had traded excessively on his account.

CONCISE RULE OF LAW: Excessive trading, or "churning," occurs when a broker buys and sells securities for a customer's account without regard to the customer's investment interests, for the purpose of generating commissions.

FACTS: Arceneaux (P) and his wife invested approximately $60,000 through the services of stockbroker Merrill Lynch, Pierce, Fenner & Smith (D). After fifteen months, Arceneaux (P) closed his account with a net loss of $45,697. During that time, the account was turned over ten times. Merrill Lynch (D) realized $11,179 in commissions. Arceneaux (P) filed suit against Merrill Lynch (D) for excessive trading, a violation of securities laws. A jury returned a verdict of $46,675 in compensatory damages and $315,000 in punitive damages. Merrill Lynch (D) appealed.

ISSUE: Does a broker violate churning laws if he buys and sells securities for a customer's account for the purpose of generating commissions?

HOLDING AND DECISION: (Fay, J.) Yes. Excessive trading, or "churning," occurs when a broker buys and sells securities for a customer's account for the purpose of generating commissions. To establish a securities churning violation, a client must prove three elements: (1) a broker's trading on a client's account is excessive in light of the client's investment objectives, (2) the broker exercised control over the account, and (3) the broker acted with intent to defraud or with willful disregard for the investor's interest. Here, the ten turnovers of Arceneaux's (P) account reflect excessive trading, Arceneaux (P) was too intimidated to contradict Merrill Lynch's (D) decisions, and the velocity of trading made no sense other than to generate commissions. While the evidence was mixed, the jury's determination that "churning" had occurred was supported by substantial evidence and will not be overturned on appeal. Affirmed.

EDITOR'S ANALYSIS: Most brokerage agreements involve a percentage commission based on the dollar value of shares traded. This creates an inherent incentive for a broker to trade a client's shares. When the broker does this mainly for his own benefit, a violation occurs.

NOTES:

R.M. PEREZ & ASSOCIATES, INC. v. WELCH
960 F.2d 534 (5th Cir. 1992).

NATURE OF CASE: Appeal of district court confirmation of an arbitration award.

FACT SUMMARY: Clients (P) of stockbroker Welch (D) signed documents containing arbitration agreements without extensive explanations of the included terms.

CONCISE RULE OF LAW: If a fraud claim relates to a contract as a whole, and the contract contains an arbitration clause, the Federal Arbitration Act requires the fraud claim to be decided by an arbitrator.

FACTS: Welch (D) was a stockbroker for Paine Webber (D). Various clients signed documents which contained arbitration clauses for any disputes with Paine Webber (D). At times, the clients were rushed to sign the documents, or did so without reading the documents thoroughly. Eight customers filed suit against Paine Webber (D) and Welch (D). Paine Webber (D) moved to require arbitration. Seven of the eight claimants were ordered to arbitration. The claims in arbitration prevailed, as did those at trial, but the claimants (P) in arbitration recovered less in damages. The claimants (P) in arbitration filed suit, challenging the requirement that they arbitrate. The district court affirmed the arbitration award, and the decision was appealed.

ISSUE: If a fraud claim relates to a contract as a whole, will an arbitration clause in the contract require the fraud claim to be decided by an arbitrator?

HOLDING AND DECISION: (Thornberry, J.) Yes. If a fraud claim relates to a contract as a whole, and the contract contains an arbitration clause, the Federal Arbitration Act requires the fraud claim to be decided by an arbitrator. If an arbitration agreement is not fraudulently made, then it is effective, even if the party to the contract did not read or understand the document. In this case, the claimants (P) do not claim that there is anything intrinsically wrong with the arbitration clauses. Instead, they complain about the entire circumstances surrounding the signing of documents. Therefore, the fraud allegations go to the formation of the entire contract, and the fraud claims were properly the subject of arbitration. Affirmed.

EDITOR'S ANALYSIS: Arbitration is often seen as an inadequate remedy when compared with trial proceedings. However, studies of arbitrated claims show that claimants do reasonably well. Given that arbitration saves money and added strain on courts, there seems to be a valuable place for arbitration in dispute resolution.

NOTES:

BATEMAN EICHLER, HILL RICHARDS, INC. v. BERNER
472 U.S. 299 (1985).

NATURE OF CASE: Review of judgment awarding damages for Rule 10b-5 violations.

FACT SUMMARY: After Berner (P) traded on false insider tips supplied by brokers at Bateman Eichler (D), Bateman Eichler (D) contended that Berner's (P) own culpability barred his private action for damages.

CONCISE RULE OF LAW: In the context of insider trading, a person whose liability is solely derivative is not as culpable as one whose breach of duty gave rise to the liability in the first place.

FACTS: Lazzaro (D) was an employee of brokerage firm Bateman Eichler, Hill Richards, Inc. (D). Falsely contending that he had inside information regarding growth prospects for a certain corporation, he induced Berner (P) and numerous other investors (P) to purchase stock in the corporation. The investors (P) later sued for violations of Rule 10b-5. Bateman Eichler (D) contended that, since the investors (P) had themselves attempted to trade on inside, albeit incorrect, information, they were barred from recovery under the in pari delicto defense. This contention was rejected by the district court and the court of appeals. The Supreme Court granted review.

ISSUE: In the context of insider trading, is a person whose liability is solely derivative as culpable as one whose breach of duty gave rise to the liability in the first place?

HOLDING AND DECISION: (Brennan, J.) No. In the context of insider trading, a person whose liability is solely derivative is not as culpable as one whose breach of duty gave rise to the liability in the first place. Traditionally, the in pari delicto defense precluded recovery by a wrongdoing plaintiff on the notion that courts should not lend aid to wrongdoers. The doctrine's vitality continues to the present. However, the doctrine will not bar a suit where (1) the defendant's wrongdoing equals or outweighs the plaintiff's and (2) allowing the suit will serve important public purposes. In the context of an insider trading situation, there are important distinctions between the relative culpabilities of tippers, securities professionals, and tippees. For example, a tippee's use of material nonpublic information does not violate § 10(b) unless the tippee owes a corresponding duty to disclose the information. The wrong by the securities professional (supplying the insider information) exceeds that of the investors, as the professional is under ethical obligations not imposed on the general public. Furthermore, insider trading will be best deterred by bringing enforcement pressures to bear on the sources of such information — corporate insiders and broker-dealers. In this case, the investors (P) may indeed have violated the securities laws, but Lazzaro (D) masterminded the scheme to manipulate the market and enticed the investors (P) into any wrongdoing. Lazzaro's actions were far more culpable. Consequently, the suit here is not barred by in pari delicto. Affirmed.

EDITOR'S ANALYSIS: This case demonstrates the importance of the "gatekeeper" role played by broker/dealers in the context of insider trading liability. Liability may even be imputed to a broker-dealer firm where one department is trading on inside information gleaned by another department. To combat interdepartmental leaks, Congress enacted an amendment to the 1934 Securities Act requiring firms to adopt procedures designed to prevent misuse.

NOTES:

CHAPTER 17
THE INVESTMENT ADVISERS AND INVESTMENT COMPANY ACTS OF 1940

QUICK REFERENCE RULES OF LAW

1. **Conduct Regulation: Section 206.** The SEC may require, without a showing of intent to deceive, that a financial advisor disclose self-dealing that may affect clients. (SEC v. Capital Gains Research Bureau, Inc.)

2. **Investment Advice, Investment Information, and the First Amendment.** A person cannot be prohibited from publishing a nonpersonalized investment newsletter merely because he is not a registered investment advisor. (Lowe v. SEC)

3. **Investment Advice, Investment Information, and the First Amendment.** The SEC may constitutionally prohibit a party from publishing self-written articles about possible investments for an undisclosed amount of compensation. (SEC v. Wall Street Publishing Institute)

4. **The Compensation of Investment Company Affiliates.** A reasonableness standard is the proper standard to evaluate whether a fund manager performed its fiduciary duty in compliance with § 36(b) of the Investment Company Act. (Gartenberg v. Merrill Lynch Asset Management, Inc.)

5. **Joint Transactions.** A pattern of officer and director investment in securities also held by their employing investment company will run afoul of Rule 17d-1. (SEC v. Midwest Technical Development Corp.)

6. **The Definitional Problem and Some Exemptions.** A company's total activities of all sorts must be considered to determine whether the company is engaged primarily in the business of investment. (SEC v. Fifth Avenue Coach Lines, Inc.)

SEC v. CAPITAL GAINS RESEARCH BUREAU, INC.
375 U.S. 180 (1963).

NATURE OF CASE: Review of order denying injunction against alleged securities laws violations.

FACT SUMMARY: The SEC (P) sought an injunction compelling Capital Gains Research Bureau, Inc. (D) to reveal to clients its practice of purchasing shares for its own account prior to recommending them.

CONCISE RULE OF LAW: The SEC may require, without a showing of intent to deceive, that a financial advisor disclose self-dealing that may affect clients.

FACTS: Capital Gains Research Bureau (D) was a registered investment advisor who repeatedly engaged in the practice of buying shares of stock it intended to recommend and then selling them after the recommendation caused the stock's value to rise. The SEC (P) filed an action seeking an injunction mandating disclosure of this practice to clients. The court of appeals held that such an injunction could not issue without a showing of intent to deceive. The Supreme Court granted review.

ISSUE: May the SEC require, without a showing of intent to deceive, that a financial advisor disclose self-dealing that may affect clients?

HOLDING AND DECISION: (Goldberg, J.) Yes. The SEC may, without a showing of intent to deceive, require that a financial advisor disclose self-dealing that may affect clients. The 1940 Investment Advisors Act proscribes "any . . . practice . . . which operates . . . as a fraud or deceit upon any client or prospective client." The language does not appear to require an intent to deceive. Beyond that, the clear intent behind the Act was to prohibit any sort of manipulation by investment advisors and to require full disclosure of material information. Clearly, self-dealing by an investment advisor with respect to recommended investments creates, at the very least, a strong potential for conflicts of interest and therefore should be disclosed. Reversed.

EDITOR'S ANALYSIS: The 1940 Investment Advisors Act was the last of the Roosevelt-era legislation that dramatically altered the securities markets. Like the better-known Securities Act and Securities Exchange Act, it was drafted to deal with perceived abuses in the securities markets. Congress, in passing the Act, intended to prevent investment advisors from taking advantage of their superior position vis-a-vis their clients. As with the other Acts, disclosure was the main vehicle for achieving this result.

NOTES:

LOWE v. SEC
472 U.S. 181 (1985).

NATURE OF CASE: Appeal from injunction prohibiting publication of securities-related newsletter.

FACT SUMMARY: The SEC (P) sought to enjoin Lowe (D) and his company from publishing general investment advice and commentary in a newsletter because they were not registered investment advisors.

CONCISE RULE OF LAW: A person cannot be prohibited from publishing a nonpersonalized investment newsletter merely because he is not a registered investment advisor.

FACTS: Lowe (D) operated Lowe Management Corp. (D), a registered investment advisor. In 1981 the SEC (P) revoked its registration after a series of convictions against Lowe (D). Subsequently, Lowe Management (D) began publishing investment-related newsletters of general circulation. The SEC (P) filed an action seeking to enjoin Lowe Management (D) from this activity due to its former registration revocation. The district court issued the injunction, and the court of appeals confirmed. The Supreme Court granted review.

ISSUE: Can a person be prohibited from publishing an investment newsletter merely because he is not a registered investment advisor?

HOLDING AND DECISION: (Stevens, J.) No. A person cannot be prohibited from publishing an investment newsletter merely because he is not a registered investment advisor. The Investment Advisers Act of 1940 gives the SEC (P) broad regulatory authority over those engaged in the investment advice business. The Act was designed to apply only to those who provide personalized advice catering to a specific client. Therefore, the Act excludes a "publisher of an bona fide newspaper, news magazine, or business or financial publication of regular or general circulation." The term "bona fide" was apparently inserted to allow regulation of single-issue "touts" or "tips" as opposed to regular newsletters. Here, Lowe Management's (D) newsletters, having regular publication dates, appear bona fide and therefore come within the statutory exclusion. Consequently, the SEC (P) did not have jurisdiction to regulate them. Reversed.

CONCURRENCE: (White, J.) To hold that publishers like Lowe (P) are not "investment advisors" as defined by the Act goes too far; the majority should merely have held that the Act may not constitutionally be applied to prevent unregistered advisors from offering general advice in publications like Lowe's (D).

EDITOR'S ANALYSIS: The SEC (P) is not totally without jurisdiction here. If the content of the publications had been false or misleading or had in some manner violated securities laws, the SEC (P) would have regained its authority to impose sanctions. The present case dealt only with powers of prior restraint.

NOTES:

SEC v. WALL STREET PUBLISHING INSTITUTE
851 F.2d 365 (D.C. Cir. 1988), cert. denied, 489 U.S. 1066 (1989)

NATURE OF CASE: Appeal from order enjoining certain publication practices.

FACT SUMMARY: Under its antitouting rules, the SEC (P) sought to enjoin Wall Street Publishing Institute (D) from carrying in its newsletter self-written articles about possible investments written by officials of the companies featured.

CONCISE RULE OF LAW: The SEC may constitutionally prohibit a party from publishing self-written articles about possible investments for an undisclosed amount of compensation.

FACTS: Wall Street Publishing Institute (D) published a monthly newsletter containing investment information and advice. Some of the articles were written by the very firms or companies featured in the article without disclosing that fact to readers. The SEC (P) filed an action seeking to enjoin WSPI (D) from this practice. The WSPI (D) raised the First Amendment as a defense. The district court entered an injunction, and the SEC (P) appealed.

ISSUE: May the SEC constitutionally prohibit a party from publishing self-written articles about possible investments?

HOLDING AND DECISION: (Silberman, J.) Yes. The SEC may constitutionally prohibit a party from publishing self-written articles about possible investments. Section 17(b) of the Securities Act prohibits the publication of a description of a security in exchange for undisclosed compensation. A self-written article, even if carried in an independent publication without the payment of an advertising fee, confers compensation on the publisher by saving writing and editorial costs. Therefore, § 17(b) applies. With respect to the First Amendment defense, the Supreme Court has held that governmental power to regulate content is greatest in a field subject to heavy governmental regulation. The securities industry is such an area, so the content regulations here are valid. Affirmed.

EDITOR'S ANALYSIS: "Commercial speech" is subject to less First Amendment protection than other forms of speech. The Court here declined to decide whether WSPI's (D) publication constituted commercial speech, although it did not see a clear fit between the commercial speech doctrine and the articles in question. It was of the opinion that the heavily regulated industry analysis obviated the need to decide this issue.

NOTES:

GARTENBERG v. MERRILL LYNCH ASSET MANAGEMENT INC.
694 F.2d 923 (2d Cir. 1982).

NATURE OF CASE: Appeal of dismissal of a derivative suit.

FACT SUMMARY: Gartenberg (P) challenged the amount of fees paid by the Merrill Lynch Ready Assets Trust (D) to the fund manager and advisor, Merrill Lynch Assets Management, Inc. (D), pursuant to § 36(b) of the Investment Company Act.

CONCISE RULE OF LAW: A reasonableness standard is the proper standard to evaluate whether a fund manager performed its fiduciary duty in compliance with § 36(b) of the Investment Company Act.

FACTS: Merrill Lynch Asset Management, Inc. (D) managed and advised the Merrill Lynch Ready Assets Trust (D), a money market fund. Merrill Lynch Asset Management, Inc. (D) charged an advisory fee which decreased as the fund assets increased. The effective rate was 0.288% of the fund's assets. The fund performed above average when compared to similar funds. Gartenberg (P), a shareholder in the Ready Assets Trust (D), filed a derivative action, claiming the fees were so high as to constitute a breach of fiduciary duty in violation of § 36(b) of the Investment Company Act. After a nonjury trial, the action was dismissed after the court found Asset Management's (D) fee to be comparable to the fees charged elsewhere in the market and thus a fair one. Gartenberg (P) appealed.

ISSUE: Is a reasonableness standard the appropriate method to evaluate whether a fund manager performed its fiduciary duty in compliance with § 36(b)?

HOLDING AND DECISION: (Mansfield, J.) Yes. A reasonableness standard is the proper standard to evaluate whether a fund manager performed its fiduciary duty in compliance with § 36(b) of Investment Company Act. To be guilty of a § 36(b) violation, the advisor-manager must charge a fee so disproportionately large that it bears no reasonable relationship to the services rendered and could not have been the product of arm's-length bargaining. To make this determination, all pertinent facts must be weighed. Examining the fees charged by other fund advisors to determine compliance with fiduciary duties, as did the district court in this case, is not an appropriate method to determine compliance. Funds are often captives of their advisors, and the entire industry could, in theory, be violating § 36(b). In this case, the evidence suggests that the advice and management was of the highest quality. Returns have been above average in the fund. While the practices of other fund managers can suggest an industry standard, the final analysis must be of the reasonableness of the fees in question. Affirmed.

EDITOR'S ANALYSIS: While a plaintiff may challenge a fee as unreasonable, theory and reality diverge. Defendants have almost always prevailed in cases such as this. While plaintiffs may charge pro-industry bias, the reality may simply be that intense competition amongst funds keeps fees at a competitive level.

NOTES:

SECURITIES AND EXCHANGE COMMISSION v. MIDWEST TECHNICAL DEVELOPMENT CORP.

[1961-1964 Transfer Binder] Fed. Sec. L. Rep. (CCH) ¶ 91,252 (D. Minn. 1963).

NATURE OF CASE: Suit claiming violations of § 17(d) of the Investment Company Act of 1940 and Rule 17d-1.

FACT SUMMARY: Officer and directors of Midwest (D), an investment company, purchased securities in which Midwest (D) had also invested.

CONCISE RULE OF LAW: A pattern of officer and director investment in securities also held by their employing investment company will run afoul of Rule 17d-1.

FACTS: Midwest Technical Development Corp. (D) was registered as a closed-end investment company. Midwest (D) would invest in new companies in the scientific fields, and then Midwest (D) would provide venture capital to these companies to maximize their value, thus raising the value of the stock in Midwest's (D) portfolio. In numerous cases, Midwest's (D) officers and directors purchased securities that had been, or soon would be, purchased by Midwest (D). The SEC (P) found violations of Rule 17d-1, which prohibits self-dealing, and filed suit.

ISSUE: Will a pattern of officer and director investment in securities also held by their employing investment company run afoul of Rule 17d-1?

HOLDING AND DECISION: (Nordbye, J.) Yes. A pattern of officer and director investment in securities also held by their employing investment company will run afoul of Rule 17d-1. Directors are not prohibited from purchasing stocks held in their investment company portfolios. However, Rule 17d-1 exists to monitor such activities for abuse of position. In this case, the situation is very difficult to evaluate. The directors and officers were all experienced investors. They owned numerous stocks aside from the Midwest (D) portfolio holdings. While many of the individual transactions appear innocent, the pattern is very suggestive of self-dealing and should have had the approval of the SEC (P) before it was established. Rule 17d-1 exists to monitor such behavior and remove temptations to breach trust. It must apply here, even though evidence of wrongful intent is not conclusive.

EDITOR'S ANALYSIS: SEC rules against self-dealing are criticized as economically inefficient. Valid business decisions become substantially more costly when any appearance of impropriety is discovered. For example, a legitimate securities acquisition may be put on hold if a director is found to hold the same securities. However, the time required for preclearance of the transaction may cause the business to miss the opportunity it discovered.

NOTES:

SECURITIES AND EXCHANGE COMMISSION v. FIFTH AVENUE COACH LINES, INC.

289 F. Supp. 3 (S.D.N.Y. 1968), aff'd, 435 F.2d 510 (2d Cir. 1970).

NATURE OF CASE: Suit seeking determination of § 3(a)(1) investment company status.

FACT SUMMARY: Fifth Avenue Coach Lines, Inc. (D), a bus line company, received $11 million for the condemnation of its property, and Fifth Avenue (D) then began investing the money in stocks and other securities.

CONCISE RULE OF LAW: A company's total activities of all sorts must be considered to determine whether the company is engaged primarily in the business of investment.

FACTS: Fifth Avenue (D) was a bus line company. Its properties were condemned by New York City, and it was awarded $11 million in compensation in October 1966. Fifth Avenue (D) used the money to purchase stocks and securities. By June 30, 1967, Fifth Avenue's (D) cash reserves had fallen to a total of $1.5 million. The remaining cash had been spent in an attempt to gain controlling interests in other companies. Determining that this behavior indicated an investment company out of compliance with regulations rather than a transportation company, the SEC (P) filed suit.

ISSUE: Must a company's total activities of all sorts be considered to determine whether the company is engaged primarily in the business of investing?

HOLDING AND DECISION: (MacLean, J.) Yes. A company's total activities of all sorts must be considered to determine whether the company is engaged primarily in the business of investment. A company which is no longer engaged in any particular business must eventually have engaged in some sort of business when it spends a huge cash reserve. The language of § 3(a)(1) of the Investment Company Act supports this activity-based approach since the language defines an investment company by what it actually does. In this case, Fifth Avenue (D) ceased being a bus line company when its properties were condemned and purchased. However, having $11 million in cash did not immediately make Fifth Avenue (D) an investment company. But by June 30, 1967, Fifth Avenue's (D) actions had transformed it into an investment company in fact. Certainly, the business did something when it spent most of the $11 million, and since it purchased stocks with much of that money, the clear inference is that it was an investment company.

EDITOR'S ANALYSIS: The test for determining investment company status under § 3(a)(1) of the Investment Company Act is fairly clear. If a company is primarily in the business of securities investment, then it is an investment company. All that must be done under the test is a factual analysis of the various activities that are conducted by the business. The purpose of the Act itself is to prevent abuses that may grow out of the unregulated power of management to use large pools of cash.

NOTES:

Notes

CHAPTER 18
TRANSNATIONAL SECURITIES FRAUD

QUICK REFERENCE RULES OF LAW

1. **Jurisdiction Based upon Effects.** The Securities Exchange Act applies to stock transactions occurring abroad when application is necessary to protect American investors. (Schoenbaum v. Firstbrook)

2. **The Second Circuit's View.** A generalized effect on the U.S. economy is insufficient to confer subject matter jurisdiction in a securities action. (Bersch v. Drexel Firestone, Inc.)

3. **An Expansive View.** The SEC may invoke federal jurisdiction over defendants committing fraud in the U.S., even if no effect is felt in the U.S. (SEC v. Kasser)

4. **A Restrictive View.** U.S. securities laws apply only when the illegal conduct occurs or originates in the U.S. in connection with the purchase and sale of securities and directly causes the harm complained of. (Zoelsch v. Arthur Andersen & Co.)

5. **Choice of Law Options. The Relevance of Foreign Law in Securities Litigation.** Forum selection and choice of law clauses in a contract will be upheld unless they are unreasonable under the circumstances. (Bonny v. The Society of Lloyd's)

SCHOENBAUM v. FIRSTBROOK
405 F.2d 200 (2d Cir. 1963), cert. denied, 395 U.S. 906 (1969)

NATURE OF CASE: Appeal from dismissal of shareholder derivative action seeking damages for fraud.

FACT SUMMARY: Aggrieved investors in Banff Oil filed a lawsuit based on American securities laws respecting a transaction occurring in Canada between Canadian companies.

CONCISE RULE OF LAW: The Securities Exchange Act applies to stock transactions occurring abroad when application is necessary to protect American investors.

FACTS: Banff Oil, Ltd. was a Canadian corporation with shares traded on the Toronto and American stock exchanges. At one point, Banff issued 500,000 new shares of stock to two Canadian companies (D) at $1.35 per share. Subsequent to this transaction, which had occurred in Canada, Banff stock went as high as $18 per share. Schoenbaum (P), a Banff shareholder, brought a derivative action contending that Banff directors (D), acting in concert with the purchasing companies (D), withheld favorable information in order to deflate Banff stock prices. The district court held that U.S. securities laws did not apply to the transaction and dismissed. Schoenbaum (P) appealed.

ISSUE: Does the Securities Exchange Act apply to stock transactions occurring abroad?

HOLDING AND DECISION: (Lumbard, J.) Yes. The Securities Exchange Act applies to stock transactions occurring abroad when application is necessary to protect American investors. If a stock is traded in the United States, extraterritorial transactions in the same stock are subject to U.S. jurisdiction. To hold otherwise would severely limit the ability of securities laws to protect the American investing public. Here, Banff stock was traded on the American Stock Exchange, which subjected it to U.S. jurisdiction. Section 30(b) of the Exchange Act exempts from reporting requirements certain foreign securities otherwise subject to U.S. jurisdiction; however, it does not limit application of § 10(b) of the Act, which is the basis of the suit here. [After having decided the jurisdictional issue, the court went on to hold, as a matter of law, that § 10(b) had not been violated in this case, so the dismissal was affirmed.]

EDITOR'S ANALYSIS: The jurisdictional basis for application of securities laws is quite broad. Any use of interstate communications invokes jurisdiction. This allows for substantial extraterritorial application of U.S. securities laws.

NOTES:

BERSCH v. DREXEL FIRESTONE, INC.
519 F.2d 974 (2d Cir. 1975), cert. denied, 423 U.S. 1018

NATURE OF CASE: Appeal from denial of motions to dismiss actions based on securities fraud.

FACT SUMMARY: Various plaintiffs in a class securities fraud action sought to predicate jurisdiction as to some causes of action on a generalized adverse affect on the U.S. economy.

CONCISE RULE OF LAW: A generalized effect on the U.S. economy is insufficient to confer subject matter jurisdiction in a securities action.

FACTS: I.O.S. Ltd. (D) engaged in three separate offerings. The offerings were made to foreign nationals (I.O.S. (D) was a Canadian corporation). Almost all the professional services rendered pursuant to the offering were done in Europe, although some accounting services were performed in the U.S. A few Americans ended up buying shares. After the offerings, the price of I.O.S. (D) stock collapsed, and a class-action § 10(b) litigation commenced. The district court denied I.O.S.'s (D) motion to dismiss for lack of subject matter jurisdiction partially on the basis that the debacle had had a general negative effect in the U.S. on attitudes about foreign investing.

ISSUE: Is a generalized adverse effect on the U.S. economy sufficient to confer subject matter jurisdiction in a securities action?

HOLDING AND DECISION: (Friendly, J.) No. A generalized adverse effect on the U.S. economy is insufficient to confer subject matter jurisdiction in a securities action. A court may find subject matter jurisdiction with respect to fraudulent acts relating to securities committed abroad only when they result in injury to purchasers in which the U.S. has an interest, such as U.S. citizens or residents. In addition, the antifraud provisions of American securities law apply to losses from securities sales to American residents living abroad if based on acts occurring in the U.S. Here, except as to the purchases by Americans, nothing else upon which to predicate jurisdiction has been offered, so jurisdiction is absent. Reversed in part, affirmed in part.

EDITOR'S ANALYSIS: There are two classes of jurisdiction relating to sales of shares in a foreign corporation to Americans. With respect to sales effected within U.S. borders, jurisdictional rules are the same as if a U.S. corporation were involved. However, if the sales were effected abroad, some of the culpable acts must have been performed in the U.S.

NOTES:

SEC v. KASSER
548 F.2d 109 (3d Cir. 1977), cert. denied, 431 U.S. 938

NATURE OF CASE: Appeal from dismissal of regulatory action based on securities laws violations.

FACT SUMMARY: The SEC (P) sought jurisdiction over Kasser (D), who masterminded a ponzi scheme spanning two continents but whose sole victim was a Canadian corporation.

CONCISE RULE OF LAW: The SEC may invoke federal jurisdiction over defendants committing fraud in the U.S., even if no effect is felt in the U.S.

FACTS: In an action filed by the SEC (P), it was alleged that Kasser (D) and those under his control fraudulently induced investments in their enterprise by Manitoba Development Fund, a Canadian concern. However, some of the acts giving rise to culpability occurred within U.S. borders. The district court dismissed, holding that U.S. securities laws had no application when extraterritorial securities transactions had no impact in the U.S., even if some acts had been performed in the U.S. The SEC (P) appealed.

ISSUE: May the SEC invoke jurisdiction of U.S. securities laws over defendants committing fraud in the U.S., even if no effect was felt in the U.S.?

HOLDING AND DECISION: (Adams, J.) Yes. The SEC may invoke jurisdiction of U.S. securities laws over defendants committing fraud in the U.S., even if no effect was felt in the U.S. It can hardly be argued that Congress intended to allow the United States to be used as a base for fashioning fraudulent securities schemes for export, even when they are peddled only to foreigners. Beyond that, sound policy reasons exist for allowing such jurisdiction. To hold otherwise might encourage reciprocal rulings in other countries, to the U.S.'s detriment. Also, allowing such suits may uncover related fraud which does affect the U.S. For these reasons, jurisdiction will be allowed.

EDITOR'S ANALYSIS: The statutory invocations of jurisdiction for the 1933 and 1934 Acts have not changed since their inception. It goes without saying that the securities industry is much more complex today than in those times. This leaves courts in the difficult position of trying to divine congressional intent regarding offshore funds when, in fact, Congress could not have foreseen their extensive development at the time of passage of the relevant legislation.

NOTES:

ZOELSCH v. ARTHUR ANDERSEN & CO.
824 F.2d 27 (D.C. Cir. 1987).

NATURE OF CASE: Appeal from dismissal of action seeking damages for securities fraud.

FACT SUMMARY: Zoelsch (P) sought to assert U.S. securities law jurisdiction over Arthur Andersen & Co. (D), an American corporation, for its conduct connected to securities fraud occurring in Germany to German investors.

CONCISE RULE OF LAW: U.S. securities laws apply only when the illegal conduct occurs or originates in the U.S. in connection with the purchase and sale of securities and directly causes the harm complained of.

FACTS: Zoelsch (P) invested in a tax shelter/real estate development. The project was audited by Arthur Andersen & Co. GmbH, a German corporation. Certain information incorporated into the audit was supplied by Arthur Andersen & Co. (AA-USA) (D), a U.S. partnership. The audit report was printed in Germany, in German, and distributed to German national Zoelsch (P) there. The investment proved unprofitable, and Zoelsch (P) brought a Rule 10b-5 suit against AA-USA (D), whose sole link to the transaction was the inclusion of its name in the audit report as a source of information. The district court dismissed for lack of subject matter jurisdiction, and Zoelsch (D) appealed.

ISSUE: Will U.S. securities laws be applied to frauds perpetrated in foreign countries against foreign investors?

HOLDING AND DECISION: (Bork, J.) No. U.S. Securities laws apply only when the illegal conduct occurs or originates in the U.S., in connection with the purchase and sale of securities and directly causes the harm complained of. As an initial matter, it is presumed that U.S. laws do not have extraterritorial effect unless Congress explicitly provides for it, which it has not done here. Also, the purpose behind the securities laws is to protect U.S. investors and the U.S. securities market, a goal not achieved by allowing essentially foreign transactions to be brought here. Although some circuits have taken an expansive view of jurisdiction for a variety of policy reasons, this sort of decision-making is best left to Congress. Consequently, this court holds that U.S. securities laws apply only when the domestic conduct comprises all the elements necessary to establish a Rule 10b-5 violation. Here, the fraud, if any, occurred in Germany. Whatever misrepresentations were made by AA-USA (D) were not made in connection with the sale of a security since only GmbH prepared the audit. Consequently, U.S. securities laws do not apply. Affirmed.

EDITOR'S ANALYSIS: A definite split on the issue of extraterritorial application of U.S. securities laws exists among the circuits. The Second Circuit and the D.C. Circuit use the restrictive standard described here. The Third, Eighth, and Ninth Circuits have accepted different formulations with less stringent jurisdictional standards, whereby any activity undertaken in this country that furthers fraud abroad can provide the basis for jurisdiction.

NOTES:

BONNY v. THE SOCIETY OF LLOYD'S
3 F.3d 156 (7th Cir. 1993), cert. denied, 114 S. Ct. 1057 (1994).

NATURE OF CASE: Appeal of dismissal of claims asserting fraud and securities law violations.

FACT SUMMARY: Bonny (P), and others, became underwriters of The Society of Lloyd's (D) insurance syndicates via contracts which contained both forum selection and choice of law clauses.

CONCISE RULE OF LAW: Forum selection and choice of law clauses in a contract will be upheld unless they are unreasonable under the circumstances.

FACTS: The Society of Lloyd's (D) operated a large insurance market. Individuals invested in Lloyd's (D) by underwriting syndicates. The underwriter was accountable for losses in the particular syndicate underwritten only, but liability was unlimited within the syndicate. Bonny (P), and others, were invited to invest in a syndicate. A contract was signed which included both forum selection and choice of law clauses requiring any litigation to take place in England. Bonny (P), and others, eventually suffered huge losses. Bonny (P) filed suit in federal district court, alleging various securities violations, but the suit was dismissed based on the forum selection clause. Bonny (P) appealed.

ISSUE: Will forum selection and choice of law clauses in a contract be upheld unless they are unreasonable under the circumstances?

HOLDING AND DECISION: (Lay, J.) Yes. Forum selection and choice of law clauses in a contract will be upheld unless they are unreasonable under the circumstances. The Supreme Court has indicated that the United States cannot effectively participate in international business if it forces all disputes to be resolved within its borders, regardless of the agreements between parties. Forum selection and choice of law clauses are "unreasonable" if (1) tainted by fraud, undue influence, or overwhelming bargaining power; (2) the selected forum is too gravely difficult or inconvenient; or (3) a strong public policy of the forum where the suit is brought would be contravened. Here, Bonny (P) has not made a sufficient showing that the clauses in question are unreasonable. The only argument advanced is that public policy considerations weigh against a waiver of Securities Act remedies. This argument is unpersuasive as England also provides remedies for securities violations. Affirmed.

EDITOR'S ANALYSIS: The current explosion in international trade will have a substantial impact on securities litigation. If American investors feel that the United States is the only acceptable forum for disputes, then they will have to negotiate such a term in any agreement. The value of such a clause will become a factor in the determination of the overall contract price.

NOTES:

Notes

the TOTAL STUDY Team

Casenote Legal Briefs

America's best selling legal briefs

Features: casenote® CASE CAPSULES
States essence of the case at a glance

▶ **COMPLETE BRIEFS** *The most comprehensive briefs; concurrences and dissents are never omitted; judge's names are included; no sketchy summaries; editor's analysis discusses case relevance.*

▶ **ALL MAJOR CASES BRIEFED** *All cases appearing in bold face titles in casebook are briefed in your CASENOTES.*

▶ **TRUE-TO-CASE EXCERPTS** *Cases are briefed according to the way in which they are edited by your casebook editor.*

▶ **FREE SUPPLEMENT UPDATE SERVICE** *CASENOTES are always made complete whenever a casebook supplement is issued.*

▶ **OVER 170 TITLES**

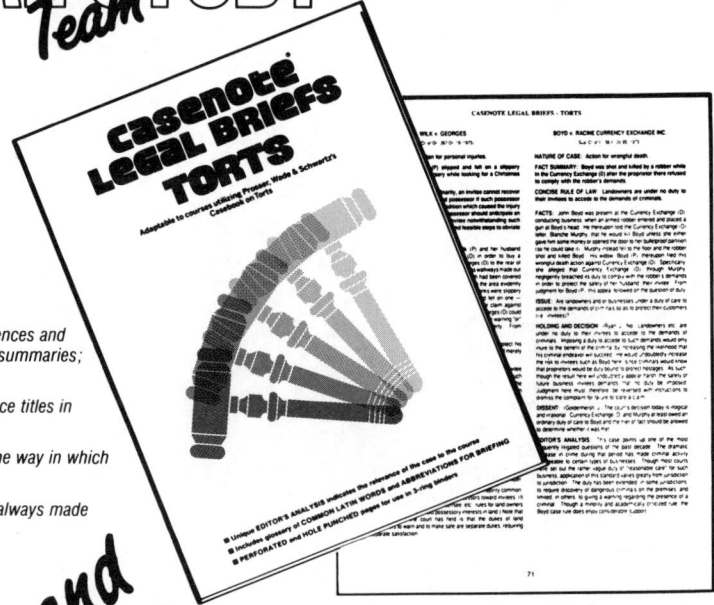

and

LAW OUTLINES from CASENOTE™

▶ *WRITTEN BY NATIONALLY RECOGNIZED AUTHORITIES IN THEIR FIELD.*

▶ *FEATURING A FLEXIBLE, SUBJECT-ORIENTED APPROACH.*

▶ *CONTAINS: TABLE OF CONTENTS; CAPSULE OUTLINE; FULL OUTLINE; EXAM PREPARATION; GLOSSARY; TABLE OF CASES; TABLE OF AUTHORITIES; CASEBOOK CROSS-REFERENCE CHART; INDEX.*

▶ *THE TOTAL LAW SUMMARY UTILIZING THE MOST COMPREHENSIVE STUDY APPROACH IN THE MOST EFFECTIVE, EASY-TO-READ FORMAT.*

the Ultimate Outline

REF #	SUBJECT	AUTHORS	RETAIL PRICE
#5260	ADMINISTRATIVE LAW	by **Charles H. Koch, Jr.,** Dudley W. Woodbridge Professor of Law, College of William and Mary. **Sidney A. Shapiro,** John M. Rounds Professor of Law, University of Kansas. (1996) w/'98 supp.)	(effective 7/1/98) $20.95
#5040	CIVIL PROCEDURE	by **John B. Oakley,** Professor of Law, University of California, Davis. **Rex R. Perschbacher,** Professor of Law & Associate Dean, Academic Affairs, University of California, Davis. (1996)	$21.95
	COMMERCIAL LAW	(*see* 5700 SALES ● 5710 SECURED TRANS. ● 5720 NEG. INSTRUMENTS & PMT. SYST.)	
#5070	CONFLICT OF LAWS	by **Luther L. McDougal, III,** W.R. Irby Professor of Law, Tulane University. **Robert L. Felix,** James P. Mozingo, III Professor of Law, University of South Carolina. (1996)	$20.95
#5080	CONSTITUTIONAL LAW	by **Gary Goodpaster,** Prof. of Law, Univ. of Calif., Davis. (1997 w/'98 supp.)	$23.95
#5010	CONTRACTS	by **Daniel Wm. Fessler,** Professor of Law, University of California, Davis. (1996)	$20.95
#5050	CORPORATIONS AND ALTERNATIVE BUSINESS VEHICLES	by **Lewis D. Solomon,** Arthur Selwin Miller Research Prof. of Law, George Washington Univ. **Daniel Wm. Fessler,** Professor of Law, University of California, Davis. **Arthur E. Wilmarth, Jr.,** Associate Professor of Law, George Washington University. (1997)	$23.95
#5020	CRIMINAL LAW	by **Joshua Dressler,** Professor of Law, McGeorge School of Law. (1996)	$20.95
#5200	CRIMINAL PROCEDURE	by **Joshua Dressler,** Prof. of Law, McGeorge School of Law. (1997)	$19.95
#5800	ESTATE & GIFT TAX INCLUDING THE FEDERAL GENERATION-SKIPPING TAX	by **Joseph M. Dodge,** W.H. Francis Professor of Law, University of Texas at Austin. (w/ supp. due Fall 1998)	$20.95
#5060	EVIDENCE	by **Kenneth Graham, Jr.,** Professor of Law, University of California, Los Angeles. (1996)	$22.95
#5400	FEDERAL COURTS	by **Howard P. Fink,** Isadore and Ida Topper Prof. of Law, Ohio State. Univ. **Linda S. Mullenix,** Bernard J. Ward Centennial Prof. of Law, Univ. of Texas. (1997)	$21.95
#5210	FEDERAL INCOME TAXATION	by **Joseph M. Dodge,** W.H. Francis Professor of Law, University of Texas at Austin (1998).	$21.95
#5300	LEGAL RESEARCH	by **Nancy L. Schultz,** Associate Professor of Law, Chapman University. **Louis J. Sirico, Jr.,** Professor of Law, Villanova University School of Law. (1996)	$20.95
#5720	NEGOTIABLE INSTRUMENTS & PMT. SYST.	by **Donald B. King,** Prof. of Law, St. Louis Univ. **Peter Winship,** James Cleo Thompson Sr. Trustee Professor, Southern Methodist University. (1995)	$21.95
#5030	PROPERTY	by **Sheldon F. Kurtz,** Percy Bordwell Professor of Law, University of Iowa, and **Patricia Cain,** Professor of Law, University of Iowa (1997).	$21.95
#5700	SALES	by **Robert E. Scott,** Dean and Lewis F. Powell, Jr. Professor of Law, University of Virginia. **Donald B. King,** Professor of Law, St. Louis University. (1992)	$20.95
#5710	SECURED TRANSACTIONS	by **Donald B. King,** Professor of Law, St. Louis Univ. (1995 w/'96 supp.)	$19.95
#5000	TORTS	by **George C. Christie,** James B. Duke Professor of Law, Duke University. **Jerry J. Phillips,** W.P. Toms Professor of Law & Chair, Committee on Admissions, University of Tennessee. (1996 w/'98 supp.)	$21.95
#5220	WILLS, TRUSTS & ESTATES	by **William M. McGovern,** Professor of Law, University of California, Los Angeles. (1996)	$21.95

rev. 1/1/98